Folger Monographs on Tudor and Stuart Civilization, No. 3

COLERIDGE ON SHAKESPEARE

The Text of the Lectures of 1811–12

COLERIDGE ON SHAKESPEARE
The text of the Lectures of 1811-12

Edited by

R. A. Foakes

Published for
The Folger Shakespeare Library
by
The University Press of Virginia
Charlottesville

THE UNIVERSITY PRESS OF VIRGINIA
Copyright © 1971 R. A. Foakes

First published 1971

The Folger Shakespeare Library is
administered by the Trustees of
Amherst College.

Standard Book Number: 8139-0340-8

Library of Congress Catalog Card Number: 78-150748

Printed in Great Britain

Contents

Illustrations

LONDON PHILOSOPHICAL SOCIETY,

SCOT'S CORPORATION HALL,

CRANE COURT, FLEET STREET,

(ENTRANCE FROM FETTER LANE.)

MR. COLERIDGE

WILL COMMENCE

ON MONDAY, NOV. 18th,

A COURSE OF LECTURES ON SHAKESPEAR AND MILTON,

IN ILLUSTRATION OF

THE PRINCIPLES OF POETRY,

AND THEIR

Application as Grounds. of Criticism to the most popular Works of later English Poets, those of the Living included.

AFTER an introductory Lecture on False Criticism, (especially in Poetry,) and on its Causes : two thirds of the remaining course, will be assigned, 1st, to a philosophic Analysis and Explanation of all the principal *Characters* of our great Dramatist, as OTHELLO, FALSTAFF, RICHARD 3d, IAGO, HAMLET, &c. : and 2nd, to a critical *Comparison* of SHAKESPEAR, in respect of Diction, Imagery, management of the Passions, Judgment in the construction of his Dramas, in short, of all that belongs to him as a Poet, and as a dramatic Poet, with his contemporaries, or immediate successors, JONSON, BEAUMONT and FLETCHER, FORD, MASSINGER, &c. in the endeavour to determine what SHAKESPEAR's Merits and Defects are common to him with other Writers of the same age, and what remain peculiar to his own Genius.

The Course will extend to fifteen Lectures, which will be given on Monday and Thursday evenings successively. The Lectures to commence at ½ past 7 o'clock.

Single Tickets for the whole Course, 2 Guineas; or 3 Guineas with the privilege of introducing a Lady: may be procured at J. Hatchard's, 190, Piccadilly; J. Murray's, Fleet Street; J. and A. Arch's, Booksellers and Stationers, Cornhill; Godwin's Juvenile Library, Skinner Street; W. Pople's, 67, Chancery Lane; or by Letter (post paid) to Mr. S. T. Coleridge, J. J. Morgan's, Esq. No. 7, Portland Place, Hammersmith.

W. Pople, Printer, Chancery Lane, London.

1   Prospectus of Coleridge's course of lectures starting on 18th November 1811 (see pp. 8 and 18).

Preface

This book has the nature of an interim report, and the material presented here will eventually appear more fully documented, and in greater detail, in the appropriate volume of the *Collected Coleridge*. A new text of the important lectures Coleridge gave on Shakespeare in 1811–12 is however sufficiently important to deserve immediate publication, since it is a considerable improvement on the text available in the standard editions of a major critic. I am sad that Mr John Crow did not live to see this edition in print; he helped with characteristic generosity to solve some of the problems I encountered. I am indebted to Professor Kathleen Coburn, Mr J. C. Maxwell, Professor M. M. Mahood, to the Bollingen Foundation, to the staffs of the Folger Shakespeare Library and the British Museum, and to Mr F. Higenbotham, for assistance in preparing this edition. The photographs of the Prospectus and the pages from Brochures 5 and 10 are reproduced by courtesy of the Folger Shakespeare Library, Washington, and the photographs of Collier's short-hand notes by courtesy of the Library of Congress, Washington.

Some advance notice of this edition has been given in my essay called 'The Text of Coleridge's 1811–12 Shakespeare Lectures', published in *Shakespeare Survey*, 23 (1970), 101–11. The passages cited there are printed exactly as written in the manuscript; in the present edition I have expanded Collier's contractions and added enough punctuation to make for ease of reading. Original footnotes are indicated by an asterisk (*), dagger (†), etc., whereas my own are numbered.

A few short forms of titles are used, and some abbreviations, but all except one are, I trust, self-explanatory. The exception is the form of reference to *Coleridge's Shakespearean Criticism*, ed. T. M. Raysor, 2 vols. (1930), and revised for the Everyman edition, also in 2 vols.

(1960). The revised edition omits some of the material printed in the first edition, which has long been out of print; but many users of this book may own or have access to the 1960 edition only. I have therefore thought it might be helpful to give page references normally to both editions in this manner: 'Raysor, II, 157 (119)'.

R. A. Foakes

I

Introduction

Samuel Taylor Coleridge did not publish the lectures he gave at various times on Shakespeare, and the most substantial and complete texts we possess relate to the series he gave in the winter of 1811–12. They were published by John Payne Collier in 1856 as *Seven Lectures on Shakespeare and Milton*. At the time, and for a few years afterwards, their authenticity was the subject of some controversy, but they have long been accepted into the canon of Coleridge's works, and comprise about two-thirds of the lecture-notes printed in vol. II of T. M. Raysor's *Coleridge's Shakespearean Criticism* in 1930, and reprinted, with slight revisions, in the Everyman series in 1960. These lectures include well-known accounts of *Romeo and Juliet* and *The Tempest*, and some remarkable comments on other plays, among them *Richard II* and *Hamlet*. They form an important part of a major critic's assessment of Shakespeare. The accuracy of the text Collier printed more than forty years after the lectures were given is a matter, therefore, of some concern. The purpose of the present book is to make available what I believe to be a better and more accurate text of these lectures than the one he published. The story that must first be told is a complicated one, and it begins with John Payne Collier.

2

He was born in 1789, the son of John Dyer Collier, at one time editor of *The Critical Review*, and later a reporter for *The Times* and the *Morning Chronicle*. His father had a wide acquaintance with literary men; Henry Crabb Robinson apparently lived with him for a time, and he knew

Charles Lamb, William Hazlitt, William Godwin, Coleridge and Wordsworth. By 1809 John Payne Collier had succeeded his father as a reporter,
and learned short-hand from him. He entered the Middle Temple in
1811, and qualified as a barrister, although he was not called to the Bar
until 1829. The reason for this was that he published *Criticisms on the
Bar* in 1819, under the quickly penetrated pseudonym of 'Amicus
Curiae'.

Probably he did not really want a career in law, but in letters. He acted
as a reporter for *The Times*, and then for the *Morning Chronicle*, on
legal, literary and dramatic matters for some years. Marriage brought
him money, and he devoted himself increasingly to literature, publishing
some poems, but turning more to scholarly and antiquarian pursuits.
The urge to concern himself with literature rather than the law may
have been stimulated by his meetings with the authors his father knew,
and by some of the reporting he did. We have Henry Crabb Robinson's
word for it that the lectures Coleridge gave in 1811–12 were reported for
the *Morning Chronicle* 'sometimes by Mr. Collier, sometimes by John
C., and sometimes by myself'.[1] At this time, it should be noted, there is
no evidence to suggest that Collier was inclined to fabricate notes and
documents; later he became notorious for doing so, but his first forgeries
appeared in his *History of Dramatic Poetry* published in 1831.

Beginning on 10 October 1811, Collier for about six weeks kept a
diary, in which he commented pretty frankly on himself, on his reading,
and on people he met. The last dated entry relates to Wednesday, 27
November 1811. This diary survives, and because it contains transcripts
of some of Coleridge's lectures, I shall comment more fully on the
nature of the manuscript a little later in connection with these.[2] Its
immediate importance is that it provides some insight into the state of
mind of a young man of great ambitions and uncertain talents, who
wished somehow to make a mark in the world. This is how the diary
opens:

Thursday October 10th—1811

I this day made a resolution to keep at least as far as lays in my power a
journal of the transactions of the day. I am now 22 years and ten months
old within a day having been born on the 11th January 1789 the Æra
of the French Revolution, as it is called, in which the Bastille at Paris
was destroyed. In that year also, I am informed, the Thames was frozen

[1] Raysor, II, 203 n. (160 n.), 211 (160), and 228 (180).
[2] See below, p. 12ff.

over. What important events marked that memorable period; but still, nonsensical as it may seem, it gives me some pleasure to think that the period at which I was born was marked by some extraordinary occurrence. To what is this feeling owing? It may be still more idle and vain to wish (yet no young mind is without ambition, or if it is, it is not as it should be) that (I cannot find modest terms so I will be plain) I should rather make the year 1789 an Æra than that I should seek for it already made. I dare say on reading over tomorrow, if I should not be ashamed to do it, I shall be disgusted with the nonsense I am writing; but however it may be, I write from the feeling of the moment, and if therefore I am ashamed of what I write I must be ashamed of my feelings.

I believe I have a large portion of Vanity, which always presumes that there is something to be vain of, and yet in many things I do not know anybody that I have a more meager opinion of than of myself. Even this Vanity itself shows my weakness. I endeavour to repress it. Connected with it is the love of praise, but thus much I will say, that praise when I do not deserve it, and when I know that I do not, has been always disgusting to me. Even in making this journal I shew it, for I have empty folly enough to imagine (for it is nothing but mere fleeting imagination) that at some time or other, even my history, and as connected with it this Diary, may be interesting to others as well as to myself—Else if this were not the case why do I not write it in short hand, which I can do, and which would save me an immensity of trouble? I wish it to be read by others as well as by myself at some distant period: that is the fact: a fact which I am weak enough to feel, but strong enough to confess. My Father keeps a Journal, and he does it in short hand. He complained today that Gibbon wrote his Diary with the obvious view of publication —I dare say it is true and certainly Gibbon is not to be commended for it. Although I do not write it in short hand, I do not write it in long hand with the obvious view of publication, for if in it there should from reading and study (which God knows I have little enough of) anything creep out of this skull of mine that may be of the least use, I wish it to be at the service of others, which it could not be if I wrote it in short hand. I am not quite certain if what I have last said be not to a certain extent somewhat contradictory to what I have before stated.

From what I have already observed it may be gathered that I have to add to vanity and the love of praise a dubiously valuable quality, which is Ambition. I say a dubiously valuable quality, because in my mind it admits of great doubt whether it be a virtue or a vice, a blessing or a curse, or whether in truth it be not both or either. I have frequently argued the question in debates, always defending Ambition perhaps somewhat too strongly, and certainly it must be admitted on all hands that a young man without ambition or emulation (which is nearly the same thing) is a pest to Society; whether he is a pest to Society or a blessing to it with Ambition may, I think, depend upon himself. Without it he is a mere burden, he is like a—I can find no comparison; to say he is like himself would be wholly illogical, and to say he is like anything else in the creation (where all have their uses) would be blasphemous. This appears like a fallacy, because I first say that an unambitious being is a pest and of no use, and then add that all created things have their uses:

> If from the Chain a single link you strike
> Tenth or ten thousandth breaks the chain alike—

but it must be observed that I by no means presume that there is such a creature as an unambitious man in the Universe: on the contrary I believe all from the highest to the lowest possess this quality, or what you please to call it, in a greater or less degree.

It is true I have begun what I have called a Diary and I have headed it with this day's date but yet though I have scrambled over five or six pages and yet I have not said a word of the occurrences of the day. The truth is I do not mean here merely (if I pursue my plan, which I may or may not do) to insert the dry details of the transactions but to intersperse what I say with my own remarks such as they are upon what I have seen, what I have heard, what I have said, or what I have done or read, and as I have done nothing, seen nothing, read nothing, and heard nothing particularly worthy of notice in this grand repository, I have filled it up with reflexions, stupid enough I really believe to everyone else but to me really and truly entertaining.

At this time Collier was, by his own account, vain enough to think well of himself, and to suppose that posterity might wish to read what he was writing; at the same time, he was conscious that what he was setting down was trivial, even 'stupid'.

The entries that follow record visits to the theatre or to church, reflections on his reading, and his reactions to company he met. It is evident that his main interests by this time were literary. He copied out long passages from the prefaces by Pope and Johnson to their editions of Shakespeare, from Thomson's *The Seasons*, from various critics on the 'origin and rise and progress of Poetry among the Romans' (entry of 22 October), from Robert Burns, and Sir John Suckling, and he spent days in November reading for the first time through Milton's *Paradise Lost* (entry of 5 November). The diary shows too that although Collier took pleasure in keeping it as 'a mode of being egotistical without being ridiculous' (entry of 13 October), and registered in it his sense of his own importance, at the same time he could be severely self-critical, as in the entry for 1 November:

I have been greatly disheartened in all my studies by many things but principally by two—1. That my memory is so bad, and 2. that my ability is so small. I say the last without the least affectation of humility; for the first I have some excuse, that my mind is so occupied from morning till night with other things, that what I have been reading, instead of being the constant subject of reflection as it naturally would be, is only forced upon my attention. I have to drive away present thoughts and to place myself in a sphere as different as light from Darkness. I feel myself wholly inadequate to the study of the Law—I feel my mind sink within me when I reflect upon it: I see an immense mountain before me at a distance which I know to be steep and of hard ascent, and which I learn from the report of those who have traversed it is full of thorny briars and obstructions of every kind—I feel my strength unequal to the task. My eye just reaches the top which from its height only serves to deter me. I am an animal that can travel a long way and very cheerfully on a plain smooth road, but I am not the patient sure footed mule that can labour up the steepest eminences, and overcome the most discouraging difficulties. And yet if I do not pursue the law what am I to follow? Am I to be a Reporter all the days of my life? Am I to drag along the valley of existence which far from being covered with luxuriance and flowers serves only as the channel of a muddy river that carries to the sea of eternity all the filth of the world—Oh no—Both ways I am defeated, or rather decline the contest.

Unhappy with both the careers available to him, law and reporting, and conscious of the limitations of his ability, Collier nevertheless had already an interest which led him in the direction he was to go; in the entry for 5 November he wrote, 'I often wish I was a poet . . . I could go on for a year on the passages that I admire, but must restrain myself.' If he was unable to be a poet, he could, and did, become a man of letters, an editor, scholar and critic. As I noted earlier, he may have been swayed in this by meeting at his father's house, or at Charles Lamb's, eminent writers of the day, and particularly Coleridge, who made an enormous impact on this impressionable young man. He first met Coleridge at some time in 1810, and recorded part of a conversation at his father's house.[1]

[1] See below, p. 30.

On 16 October 1811, he met Coleridge at Lamb's house, intending to set down all Coleridge said, and was overcome: 'I went into the room where he and many more were at ½ past 8, and before a quarter past 9 my mind was so burdened with the things worthy of recollection that he said that I was obliged to relieve myself by quitting his company.' A few days later he began the entry in his diary, 'This day I again had the delight of being in company with the greatest man of the present day, and in some respects unrivalled in any former age'; he went on that evening and the next morning to set down what he remembered of Coleridge's conversation, and it is hardly surprising that in this condition of hero-worship Collier attended the course of lectures Coleridge commenced on Monday, 18 November 1811. After the first two, he returned home and immediately transcribed in long-hand into his diary the notes he had taken of the lectures, heading the second, on 21 November:

> This evening Coleridge delivered his second Lecture, which is not only beyond my praise, but beyond the praise of any man, but himself. He only is capable of speaking of himself. All others seem so contemptible in comparison. I felt myself more humble if possible than the meanest worm before the Almighty, and blessed my stars that I could comprehend what he had the power to invent.[1]

It is reasonable to suppose that, being in this frame of mind, Collier sought to set down faithfully and accurately what Coleridge said.

3

It is important to keep in mind this image of the young, uncertain, hero-worshipping Collier, overwhelmed in the presence of the genius, Coleridge, and trying, as he said,[2] to set down 'everything that he said worthy of recollection'. For the diary dropped out of sight, and the next episode in the story begins in 1854, when Collier, now a mature scholar in his sixties, moved house in Maidenhead. It was then, according to the preface he wrote to *Seven Lectures on Shakespeare and Milton by the late S. T. Coleridge* (1856), that he found a set of short-hand notes he had taken more than forty years earlier at the lectures Coleridge gave on Shakespeare and other poets in 1811–12. He also discovered 'transcripts

---

[1] See below, p. 52.
[2] See below, p. 31.

2 Two pages from brochure 5; the text, from Lecture 6, is printed on pp. 64-5.

3 Two pages from brochure 10; the text, from Lecture 12, is printed on pp. 122-3. The pencilled interlineation 'See short-hand Note A' shows faintly on the second page, four lines from the bottom (see pp. 18-19).

in long-hand of some of the said notes', on turning out a 'double chest of drawers', although diligent search on a number of previous occasions had failed to locate them.[1] Collier announced his discovery in a series of four short contributions to *Notes and Queries* in July and August 1854; it was the first intimation to the world that a substantial text for a number of the lectures had survived. In the first two pieces in this periodical he printed excerpts said to be from a diary he had kept at the time he attended the lectures, stating that 'only fragments remain' of it,[2] and he also reprinted the prospectuses of the series of lectures given by Coleridge in 1811–12 and in 1818. In the last two pieces he included some passages from his notes of the lectures. His 'memoranda' of seven lectures (Nos. 1, 2, 6, 7, 8 and 9 of the seventeen Coleridge delivered in the series) he claimed were 'generally very full, and in the *ipsissima verba* of the author'.[3]

Collier's story, that he had mislaid his short-hand notes for more than forty years, is probably true, but his announcement of his find in 1854, and his subsequent publication of the lectures in 1856, were nicely timed to supplement Sara Coleridge's collection of her father's *Notes and Lectures upon Shakespeare* (1849). By the 1850s Collier had made a reputation as a scholar and antiquarian; he had also, especially after the publication in 1852 of the manuscript notes and emendations he claimed to have found in a copy of the Second Folio of Shakespeare's plays, begun to acquire some notoriety as a fabricator, and a man whose word was unreliable.[4] The man who could forge marginalia in the so-called 'Perkins' Folio, and claim them as original emendations of Shakespeare's text, might equally fabricate or emend the text of Coleridge. Collier was no longer the young hero-worshipper, anxious to record the very words uttered by a great poet. His contributions to *Notes and Queries* received favourable notice in *The Athenaeum*, the editor of which, W. H. Dixon, like Collier himself an antiquary and lawyer, remained his loyal supporter, and refused to print a hostile letter submitted to him.

This letter was subsequently published as a pamphlet called *Literary Cookery with Reference to Matters attributed to Coleridge and Shakespeare* (1855), and it is devoted mainly to a demonstration, by reference to

---

[1] Preface to *Seven Lectures*, iii, xi.

[2] *Notes and Queries*, X (July–August, 1854), 2.

[3] Ibid., 1.

[4] A good brief account of Collier's fabrications relating to Shakespeare is given in E. K. Chambers, *William Shakespeare, A Study of Facts and Problems* (1930), II, 384–93.

James Gillman's *Life of Coleridge*, that the prospectus which Collier said was published in 1812 in fact appeared in 1811. This was an oversight on Collier's part; the prospectus Coleridge issued late in 1811 for the course of lectures he gave in the winter of 1811–12 bears no date,[1] and Collier had not troubled to check when it was issued. Nevertheless, the insinuations of this pamphlet, written by Andrew Edmund Brae, but published under the pseudonym, 'A Detective', irritated Collier sufficiently to tempt him to initiate proceedings for libel, and in January 1856 he moved for a criminal information against the publisher of it. On 8 January he swore an affidavit in the Court of Queen's Bench recounting the history of his attendance at Coleridge's lectures, and the story of how he had lost his notes and then recovered them in 1854. In support of his affidavit, he entered various documents at the Court, which were marked with capital letters to identify them, and signed by an officer of the Court. The proposed suit for libel went no further than this.[2]

Later in the same year (the dedication is dated 10 July 1856) Collier published *Seven Lectures on Shakespeare and Milton*. A full text of the lectures from which excerpts had been printed in *Notes and Queries* occupies about half the volume. To make a large book, Collier added a reprint of the notes and emendations from the 'Perkins' Folio of Shakespeare, which occupy the last 125 pages. A substantial preface is devoted partly to the Coleridge material, and partly to a defence of the notes on Shakespeare. These had already been the subject of much discussion, and had been attacked as spurious by a number of scholars, including J. O. Halliwell and S. W. Singer.[3] Collier could rely on the support of *The Athenaeum*, and of some Shakespearians, and could crow a little in the preface over Singer, who had changed his mind, and had come to accept some of the emendations as genuine. However, the weight of the evidence was against him, and after a further sharp attack on him by Alexander Dyce in 1859, Collier's claims were utterly demolished by C. M. Ingleby in his *A Complete View of the Shakespeare Controversy* (1861). In this book Dr Ingleby showed, in a recapitulation of the whole affair, that the emendations in the Shakespeare Folio had been fabricated, and were written in Collier's own hand.

The matter of the Shakespeare emendations had been so large an

---

[1] The Prospectus is reprinted above, p. viii.

[2] Collier reprinted the affidavit, with comments on the proposed suit for libel, in the Preface to *Seven Lectures*, i–v.

[3] See J. O. Halliwell, *Curiosities of Modern Shakespearian Criticism* (1853), and S. W. Singer, *The Text of Shakespeare Vindicated* (1853).

issue and had drawn so much attention,[1] that the authenticity of the text of the Coleridge lectures seemed almost trivial by comparison. Dr Ingleby gave little space to these, as he in any case felt sure that 'the finishing stroke in the demolition of the genuineness of the "Seven Lectures", which Mr. Collier in 1856 published as Coleridge's' had already been delivered. The final blow, he thought, had been given in *Collier, Coleridge and Shakespeare. A Review*, published in 1860 as by the author of *Literary Cookery*. In the event he was quite mistaken, for as the controversy stimulated by the publication of Collier's *Seven Lectures* (1856) faded away, some evidence appeared to validate Collier's claims about these. In 1869 extracts from the diary and correspondence of Henry Crabb Robinson were published, confirming that Collier had indeed attended the lectures Coleridge gave in 1811–12, and helping to authenticate parts of his text. Furthermore, the reports of the lectures which had been printed in *Morning Chronicle* were discovered, and these also tended to bear out Collier's claim to be presenting a true text of the lectures. When Thomas Ashe gathered Coleridge's notes and lectures on Shakespeare and other poets for publication in Bohn's Library in 1883, he was pleased to be able to reprint much of Collier's Preface, and all the text of the lectures as these were printed in 1856, together with extracts from Crabb Robinson's Diary, and the reports from the *Morning Chronicle*. By the time T. M. Raysor came to publish his definitive edition of Coleridge's *Shakespearean Criticism* in 1930, he had learned that Collier himself was responsible for some of the reports in the *Morning Chronicle*, and he could see no reason for troubling to defend the authenticity of Collier's text. Indeed, he was able to add further corroboration by pointing to a number of links and overlaps between Collier's text and various authentic fragmentary manuscript notes by Coleridge now printed for the first time.[2]

4

The text offered by Collier in *Seven Lectures on Shakespeare and Milton* has, then, been accepted into the canon of Coleridge's works, and provides the only substantial record we possess of the lectures he gave on

---

[1] In his book, pp. 339–48, Ingleby printed an annotated list of twenty-two books and pamphlets, and references to a number of essays in periodicals, published between 1852 and 1860 relating to the controversy aroused by the publication of Collier's emendations to Shakespeare.

[2] See Raysor, II, 25 (22).

Shakespeare. Raysor argued, reasonably enough, that to suppose Collier invented lectures so 'characteristic of Coleridge in his greatest excellences as well as his faults is to attribute to the great literary forger genius rather than dishonesty'.[1] However, a study of *Collier, Coleridge and Shakespeare* shows that the matter is not quite so straightforward. Although the author of this, Andrew Brae,[2] was not able to substantiate the charges he made of 'literary fraud' and 'fabrication' against Collier in respect of the Coleridge material, he succeeded in exposing some absurdities and disturbing features in Collier's text, often by comparing passages from *Seven Lectures* with passages on similar themes in Coleridge's *Literary Remains*, edited by H. N. Coleridge in 1836. Coleridge sometimes used the same material in a variety of contexts, but with differences of wording, so that similarities may provide inconclusive textual evidence, and Andrew Brae pressed some trivial points too hard. At the same time, he had a sharp critical eye, as, for example, in his comments on a passage in Lecture 6: he noticed that, according to Collier, Coleridge said:[3]

> Not long since, when I lectured at the Royal Institution, I had the honour of sitting at the desk so ably occupied by Sir Humphry Davy, who may be said to have elevated the art of chemistry to the dignity of a science.

Now Brae could show that Humphry Davy was knighted some months after this lecture was delivered, so that Coleridge would certainly not have referred to '*Sir* Humphry Davy';[4] but, in addition, he pointed to the absurdity of the wording here, and asked, 'Who, that knows anything of the history of chemistry, could believe that Coleridge ever said anything so silly as that *the art* of chemistry might be said to have been elevated in

---

[1] Ibid., II, 25 (22).

[2] Andrew Edmund Brae died in old age in December 1881, and is the subject of an obituary by C. M. Ingleby in *Notes and Queries*, 6th Series, VI (21 October 1882), 323–4. He published a number of notes and papers, on Chaucer and Shakespeare principally, and wrote a commentary on *The Tempest* (see the further note by Ingleby in *Notes and Queries*, 6th series, IX (17 May 1884), 396). His earliest note on Shakespeare seems to be one on *The Tempest*, published in *Notes and Queries*, II (19 October 1850), 338. Although he published *Collier, Coleridge and Shakespeare* anonymously, his authorship of it was known to C. M. Ingleby by the time he brought out *A Complete View of the Shakespeare Controversy* in 1861.

[3] *Seven Lectures*, 31; Raysor, II, 113 (82). See also below, p. 65.

[4] *Collier, Coleridge and Shakespeare*, 41. The lecture was delivered on 5 December 1811: Davy was knighted in April 1812.

the nineteenth century to the dignity of *a science*?'[1] The question is a reasonable one, and although Brae's criticisms are not often as well judged as this, and sometimes reveal his own failure to appreciate Coleridge's subtlety, as in the analysis of *The Tempest* in Lecture 9, nevertheless there is enough substance in his argument to cast considerable doubt on Collier's claims.

Not that it is a simple matter to determine just what Collier was claiming to do, for he says a number of different, and to some extent contradictory, things; and Brae was responding to the most confident of Collier's assertions, notably his statement in *Notes and Queries* in 1854 that the 'memoranda' he had found of seven of Coleridge's lectures were 'generally very full, and in the *ipsissima verba* of the author'.[2] In the Preface to *Seven Lectures on Shakespeare and Milton* in 1856, Collier modified these words. He used the same phrase again, but with qualification, and about some passages he claimed to be quoting from his Diary for October 1811: 'That these were Coleridge's *ipsissima verba* I cannot, at this distance of time, state; but they are the *ipsissima verba* in my Diary.'[3] About the lectures themselves Collier's claims were also more modest, if not very clear or consistent, in 1856. At one point he asserted:[4]

I am certain, even at this distance of time, that I did not knowingly register a sentence, that did not come from Coleridge's lips, although doubtless I missed, omitted, and mistook points and passages, which now I should have been most rejoiced to have preserved. In completing my transcripts, however, I have added no word or syllable of my own.

A little later he seems to contradict this last sentence, confessing, 'in some cases I relied upon my recollection to fill up chasms in my memoranda',[5] the recollection, that is, of words spoken forty-five years previously. Then, too, he acknowledged that while he took down his notes in the third person, he has put them all into the first person to make them 'consistent with each other':[6] but again he states, 'I present my notes merely as they are.'[7] He does not seem to have had a clear conception of what he was doing, and Brae's demonstration that the 'Sir'

---

1 Ibid., 42.
2 *Notes and Queries*, X (July–August, 1854), 1.
3 *Seven Lectures*, Preface, xxv.
4 Ibid., vi–vii.
5 Ibid., xiii.
6 Ibid., xiii.
7 Ibid., xiii.

given to Humphry Davy must be a later addition in itself seriously undermines Collier's claim to have added 'no word or syllable of my own'.

The question raised by all this is not whether Collier fabricated the lectures, as Brae and Ingleby thought, for so much in them is characteristic of Coleridge that Raysor's argument stands: if Collier invented them, he was a genius. The question is rather, just how much did Collier alter, rewrite, or add to, his original notes? Just what kind of text does the 1856 edition provide? It is also proper to ask whether Andrew Brae was justified in asserting that the reader of Collier's versions would 'seek in vain for that vivid and peculiar phraseology he has been accustomed to associate with Coleridge'.[1] For by the 1850s Collier was certainly capable of rewriting Coleridge's words, and tampering freely with them, whatever claims he was making for accuracy; the mature Collier is judiciously described by G. F. Warner in the *Dictionary of National Biography*, where he warns, 'None of his statements or quotations can be trusted without verifying, and no volume or document that passed through his hands can be too carefully scrutinised.'[2]

5

In the Preface to *Seven Lectures on Shakespeare and Milton*, Collier included the text of the affidavit he swore in the Court of Queen's Bench in January 1856. In this he says that on moving house in 1854 he recovered 'the original notes' of seven lectures, 'and also transcripts in long-hand of some of the said notes'.[3] He also found 'fragments of a diary of mine, which is now shown to me, and marked B'.[4] Later he spoke of 'fragments of a Diary in my own handwriting', and 'partial transcripts, in long-hand, of Coleridge's first, second, sixth, and eighth lectures'. He also said that the short-hand notes of Lectures 9 and 12 'were complete, but entirely untranscribed'.[5] He then prepared the text for his edition:[6]

I had employed myself in collating my early transcripts with such of the original short-hand notes as I had recovered, and in transcribing

[1] *Collier, Coleridge and Shakespeare*, 19.
[2] *Dictionary of National Biography*, XI (1887), 351.
[3] *Seven Lectures*, Preface, iii.
[4] Ibid., iii.
[5] Ibid., xii.
[6] Ibid., xii–xiii.

the ninth and twelfth Lectures, which still remained in their original state. The early transcripts were not in the first person: they, as it were, narrated the observations and criticisms of Coleridge, with constant repetitions of 'he said', 'he remarked', 'he quoted', etc. On the other hand, my original notes, taken down from the lips of the Lecturer, were, of course, in the first person,—'I beg to observe', 'it is my opinion', 'we are struck', etc. I therefore re-wrote the whole, comparing my recovered transcripts with my short-hand notes (where I had them) as I proceeded, and putting the earliest Lectures, as well as the latest, in the first instead of the third person.

Having done this, he then 'destroyed the original short-hand notes'[1] of the lectures, except for the notes of two of them, which he produced to support his affidavit, and which were marked G and H by the Court.[2]

This account of what Collier did has been generally accepted, and his statements are reprinted in T. M. Raysor's edition; however, Raysor completed his edition before the opening of the Folger Shakespeare Library in 1933, and did not check the materials there when he revised his *Coleridge's Shakespearean Criticism* in 1960.[3] That library possesses Collier's original long-hand Diary and transcripts of Coleridge's lectures. The documents consist of ten sewn gatherings or brochures, to use Collier's word, having varying numbers of pages measuring about seven and quarter by four inches; the first page of Brochure 3 has the mark 'B' on it, and a note stating that it is the Diary referred to in Collier's affidavit of January 1856.[4] The Diary proper occupies most of the first four brochures, the last ten leaves of Brochure 4 being blank. The entries in the Diary, from which some extracts have been quoted,[5] extend from 10 October to 27 November 1811. At this point Collier appears to have ceased to keep it. The pages of these four brochures are numbered continuously to p. 177, just before the entries cease, and Collier provided a fairly elaborate list of contents for each of the first three brochures. The diary entries, which include transcripts of Coleridge's first two lectures, seem to be complete for the period covered, and his description of them in 1856 as 'fragments' is, to say the least, misleading.

---

[1] Ibid., iv.
[2] Ibid., iv.
[3] This is the familiar Everyman edition, in which Raysor made certain important minor revisions, and was able to consult some manuscripts he had not seen for the 1930 edition.
[4] A full description of this manuscript is given in Appendix B; see below p. 154.
[5] See above, pp. 2–5.

The remaining six brochures contain long-hand transcripts of Lectures 6, 7, 8, 9 and 12. The handwriting appears to be virtually identical with that in the Diary, as far as a point towards the end of Lecture 12, when some kind of break in the flow of writing occurred. At this point Collier seems to have paused in his transcribing, and when he resumed he wrote in a more slanting and rapid hand, in a different ink, and turned the brochure round, writing lengthwise across the page.[1] A flurry of deletions and interlineations might indicate initial difficulties for him in taking up the long-hand transcription again at this point. These transcripts are substantial and full, with only occasional gaps where a word or phrase has been omitted. Nothing in them bears out Collier's description of them in 1856 as 'partial transcripts'. It is true that the text he published in *Seven Lectures on Shakespeare and Milton* often expands the material in these transcripts, but not in ways that affect the substance of what Coleridge was saying. The brochures clearly contain a different text from the one Collier printed.

The survival of this manuscript proves that Collier's account of the brochures is inaccurate. He said in his preface that the short-hand notes of Lectures 9 and 12 were 'entirely untranscribed', but the brochures provide a transcription of these lectures that differs continuously from the text he printed, and clearly belongs with the transcriptions of the other lectures. Possibly Collier did not intend to mislead, and did not fully realize how little relation what he was claiming to do bore to what he was actually doing. The same habit of mind is reflected in his treatment of the text. Perhaps it would be more correct to say 'texts', for in *Seven Lectures on Shakespeare and Milton* he printed, according to his own account, substantial extracts from his Diary, as well as the text of the lectures. Collier stated that he was making 'a few quotations in the words I find written with my own hand about five-and-forty years ago',[2] and then said he was citing 'the *ipsissima verba* in my Diary'.[3] In fact he rewrote his Diary, expanded it, and made all kinds of additions not in the original. Two short passages will illustrate this; in each case the text of the manuscript is followed by the text as printed in 1856:[4]

    1 (a) Coleridge is a man very fond of the display of his abilities, and perhaps very naturally and I am sure very usefully so—for no one

---

[1] See the reproduction on Plate 1.

[2] *Seven Lectures*, Preface, xiv.

[3] Ibid., xxv.

[4] For the contexts of these passages, see below, pp. 30 and 33; see also Raysor, II, 30 and 36. These passages were not included in Raysor's Everyman edition.

can hear him speak if he be ever such a dolt but must improve
by what he says. After supper on the night when he said what I have
related of Falstaff he was most entertaining indeed. No one spoke
but he, and no one wished to speak, indeed he kept us on the
continual listen and laugh so that it was almost impossible.

1 (b) As Coleridge is a man of genius and knowledge, he seems glad of
opportunities of display: being a good talker, he likes to get hold
of a good listener: he admits it, and told us the anecdote of some
very talkative Frenchman, who was introduced to a dumb lady,
who, however, politely appeared to hear all her loquacious visitor
said. When this visitor afterwards met the friend who had
introduced him, he expressed his obligation to that friend for
bringing him acquainted with so very agreeable and intelligent a
woman, and was astonished and chagrined when he was told that
she was dumb!

2 (a) [Coleridge was speaking of the recently published poem *The
Curse of Kehama* by Robert Southey]
He thought it a work of great talent but not so much genius, and he
drew the distinction between talent and genius that there is
between a Watch and an Eye: each were beautiful in their way, but
the one was made, the other grew. Talent was a manufactured
thing: genius was born.

2 (b) He looked upon 'The Curse of Kehama' as a work of great
talent, but not of much genius; and he drew the distinction between
talent and genius by comparing the first to a watch, and the last to
an eye: both were beautiful, but one was only a piece of ingenious
mechanism, while the other was a production above all art. Talent
was a manufacture; genius a gift, that no labour nor study could
supply: nobody could make an eye, but anybody, duly instructed,
could make a watch.

The first passage Collier simply rewrote, adding the anecdote of the
Frenchman, which is not in the manuscript. He may have incorporated
a story Coleridge told in conversation, and he took down, at some other
time, but the passage shows how far Collier departed from the *'ipsissima
verba'* of his own Diary in 1856. The second passage shows Collier
expanding a comment of Coleridge in such a way as to justify Andrew
Brae's complaint; what in the manuscript seems a record of Coleridge's
'vivid and peculiar phraseology' is altered so that the characteristic
opposition of the mechanical and the organic is sadly weakened.

If Collier could so change the wording of his own Diary, add new material, expand and rewrite, while claiming to quote it verbatim, it would be reasonable to suppose that he might take liberties just as great, or greater, with the text of Coleridge's lectures. The brochures containing transcripts made soon after Collier heard the lectures, confirm that he did indeed alter and expand these in a variety of ways. No authoritative text for these lectures survives in Coleridge's hand, apart from one or two fragmentary notes, so there is no way of proving how close the manuscript text of the brochures is to what Coleridge actually said, except possibly for Lectures 9 and 12, for which some further evidence is available.[1] However, I have tried to show that as a young man Collier looked on Coleridge as a kind of superior being, and was anxious to preserve his words; also, he was reporting some of the lectures for the *Morning Chronicle*, so that there are good reasons for thinking that he tried to take them down accurately. By 1856 he was a mature scholar, who had been involved in fabrications of Shakespearian material for some years, and who was bringing out lectures by a poet who had died more than twenty years previously; so that his treatment now in a cavalier way of Coleridge's text is more understandable.

In any case, the internal evidence is convincing enough, as two examples will show. One is the passage noted by Andrew Brae, and quoted above;[2] here it is again, first as it appears in the manuscript, and then as it appears in the 1856 text:

(a) Coleridge then paid a high compliment to Davy (at whose desk he had had the honour of lecturing—at the Royal Institution) who had reduced the art of Chemistry to a science.

(b) Not long since, when I lectured at the Royal Institution, I had the honour of sitting at the desk so ably occupied by Sir Humphry Davy, who may be said to have elevated the art of chemistry to the dignity of a science.

Davy was not a knight when Coleridge gave the lecture, and this indicates that the first version is closer to what Coleridge said; but in addition, the first version clarifies what he meant, namely, that Davy had given method and discipline to chemistry. When he rewrote the passage in 1856, Collier may have changed 'reduced' to 'elevated' to prevent possible misunder-

---

[1] For discussion of this, see below, pp. 158–66.
[2] See above, p. 10. For the context of the passage, which is from Lecture 6, see below, p. 65, and Raysor, II, 113 (82).

standing by Victorian readers for whom 'reduced' might have meant 'brought down to a lower condition'; but whatever his design, he effectively altered the sense.

The second passage also bears on the dating of the manuscript in relation to the 1856 text; again the version in the manuscript is given first.[1]

(a) Careless he [i.e. Shakespeare] might be, or he might write at a time when his better genius did not attend him, but he never wrote anything that he knew would degrade himself. Were it so, as well might a man pride himself on acting the beast, or a Catalani, because she did not feel in a mood to sing, begin to bray.

(b) Careless he might be, and his better genius may not always have attended him; but I fearlessly say, that he never penned a line that he knew would degrade him. No man does anything equally well at all times; but because Shakespeare could not always be the greatest of poets, was he therefore to condescend to make himself the least?

Angelica Catalani, an Italian soprano, had a great vogue in London for some years after her debut there in 1806, so that the reference to her would have been topical in 1811. Possibly Collier removed the reference to her in 1856 because it no longer had an immediate point for readers then; but whatever his reasons for making this change, his addition of a note here seems merely gratuitous. It reads as follows:

It is certain that my short-hand note in this place affords another instance of mishearing: it runs literally thus—'but because Shakespeare could not always be the greatest of poets, was he therefore to condescend to make himself a beast?' For 'a beast' we must read *the least*, the antithesis being between 'greatest' and 'least', and not between 'poet' and 'beast'.

This note seems designed to add a touch of authenticity to the presentation of his text in 1856, and at least it confirms that the original reading was 'beast'. Both of the examples cited here provide evidence that the manuscript is close to the text of the lectures as Coleridge delivered them, and illustrate the free way in which Collier altered and revised that text in *Seven Lectures on Shakespeare and Milton* in 1856.

---

[1] For the context, see below, p. 103 and n., and Raysor, II, 164 (126).

6

The question remains just how close the text of the manuscript brochures is to the lectures as Coleridge delivered them. No full answer can be given, but some further evidence needs to be taken into account at this point. In the brochures, transcripts of the first two lectures occur as part of the diary. The entry for 18 November begins, 'This afternoon Coleridge delivered his first lecture . . . I shall merely insert the notes I took of the Lecture', and on 21 November Collier wrote, 'This evening Coleridge delivered his second Lecture . . . let Coleridge speak for himself.'[1] These transcriptions were clearly made on the day the lectures were given, and, in the case of Lecture 2, partly on the following day.[2] The Diary records his attendance at Lecture 3 on 25 November, and that he immediately transcribed his notes; but in some other book or papers now lost. Entries in the Diary cease on 27 November 1811, the day before Lecture 4 was delivered, and the rest of Brochure 4 is blank. Brochure 5 is headed 'Coleridge's Sixth Lecture', and transcripts of Lectures 6, 7, 8, 9 and 12 fill the rest of the brochures, leaving blank leaves at the end of Brochure 7 (where Lecture 8 remains unfinished), in Brochure 9 after the completion of Lecture 9, and at the end of Brochure 10, which contains Lecture 12.

In the affidavit printed in *Seven Lectures on Shakespeare and Milton*, Collier said, 'In the year 1811, I attended each of a course of fifteen lectures given by the late Samuel Taylor Coleridge.'[3] He was probably quoting the figure mentioned in the Prospectus, which he reprinted in his 1856 volume. In fact, Coleridge gave seventeen lectures, so that Collier's statement is incorrect. We know for certain only that he attended Lectures 1, 2, 3, 6, 7, 8, 9 and 12. We know, too, that he transcribed the first three lectures almost immediately after hearing them. The handwriting, paper, watermarks, and internal evidence all suggest that the transcriptions of the others were also made soon after he heard them.

However, as I noted earlier,[4] at a point about two-thirds of the way through Lecture 12, the handwriting and ink change, and it appears that Collier stopped transcribing and resumed at a later date. There's nothing to indicate how much later, except for a reference to Malone's

---

[1] For the context, see below, pp. 45 and 52.

[2] See the entry for 22 November 1811, p. 59.

[3] *Seven Lectures*, Preface, iii.

[4] See above, p. 14, and for the context, see Lecture 12 below, p. 123 and n.

edition of Shakespeare published in 1821; but this is interlined, and could have been added after the transcription was finished.[1] The text Collier printed in 1856 differs continuously in detail, and sometimes in substance, from all the text as transcribed in the brochures, including the last part of Lecture 12. My guess is that Collier transcribed the bulk of the lectures soon after they were delivered, not necessarily within a day, but certainly while they were fresh in his mind; that he paused in the middle of Lecture 12, and resumed after an interval possibly of weeks or even months; and that some time after all were finished, he went back over them and made a number of corrections and interlineations, like the reference to Malone's Shakespeare.

Collier entered a number of documents in support of his affidavit of January 1856, which were marked with letters by an officer of the Court of Queen's Bench. These letters, according to the affidavit, ran from A to K, and for the most part were marked on pamphlets and books, as C, D, E and F were inscribed on issues of *Notes and Queries* for 1854. Three manuscripts were produced at the Court, one being the Diary, which has the letter 'B' on the first page of Brochure 3. It is not clear whether all ten brochures were submitted, but since they belong together, and survive as a whole, it is likely that they were. The other two manuscripts were short-hand notebooks, marked G and H; Collier said, 'After I had completed the transcripts of the said lectures [i.e. for his 1856 text], I destroyed the original short-hand notes thereof, as being of no value, except the two now produced to me, and marked G and H, which are the original notes taken down by me, from the mouth of the said Samuel Taylor Coleridge, in the year 1811.'[2] These two notebooks apparently survive, though I do not know where they are at the present time. However, in 1937, when they were owned by an American scholar, photostats were made of them, and sets were deposited in the Library of Congress and in the Folger Shakespeare Library, both in Washington, D.C.[3] The photostats show the mark 'A' written in the margin in the middle of Lecture 12, at a point roughly corresponding to the words 'See short-hand note A' in the transcript of this lecture in Brochure 10, thus confirming that the transcripts in the brochures are based on these short-hand notes.

---

[1] See below, p. 127 and n.

[2] *Seven Lectures*, Preface, iii–iv.

[3] Professor Paul Kaufman of Seattle, who had the manuscripts when the photostats were made, subsequently sold them, and does not know who the present owners are.

Collier said that he learned short-hand from his father 'at an early age',[1] and he seems to have acquired a personal variant of the system developed by John Byrom in the eighteenth century, and popularized by T. Molineux in publications like *An Introduction to Mr. Byrom's Universal English Short Hand* (1804).[2] Like most systems, including Pitman's introduced in 1837, Byrom's provides primarily a pattern of signs for consonants, and when Collier was taking down Coleridge's words at speed, he indicated few vowels and hardly any punctuation. Some of the signs he used for consonants are quite different from those of Byrom, and in addition, he used special signs for prefixes and terminations all of which it would be difficult now to recover. By its nature Collier's short-hand offers ambiguities of interpretation, as, for example, the signs for 'fct' represent 'effect', but could be read as 'fact', 'mnd' represents 'mind', but could be 'mend'; 'mn' seems to indicate 'immense', but could be read as a number of words; and 'mst' may be 'mast' or 'must'. These examples all occur early in Lecture 9.[3]

In other words, it would be a very great labour indeed to recover the whole meaning of Collier's short-hand now. It would be possible to transcribe a good deal of it, leaving gaps and numerous uncertainties and ambiguities. A study of the opening pages of Lecture 9 seems to show that Collier's short-hand was not so expert that he could take down all that Coleridge said; he appears to have set down some entire sentences, but others are recorded in abbreviated form, and some possibly not at all. His short-hand notes, in other words, are essentially a set of clues from which, with the aid of his memory, Collier could reconstruct what Coleridge said, often, but by no means at all points, in the original words. A rough transcription of the opening pages of the short-hand notes of Lecture 9 shows that these are the notes from which the transcription in the brochures was made. The transcription there is a polished version, not a literal rendering, and it shows some minor alterations, as, for example, 'in all but one respect' becomes 'in all respects but one'; 'The advantage is vast indeed on the side of the modern' becomes 'The advantage is indeed vastly on the side of the modern'; and when Coleridge was commenting on the unities in drama, the short-hand notes are very abbreviated, but show that he referred to the passage of

---

[1] *Seven Lectures*, Preface, v.

[2] In these remarks, and what follows on the short-hand notes, I have leaned heavily on the expert advice of Mr F. Higenbotham, Librarian of Canterbury City Libraries, who has made a special study of old systems of short-hand.

[3] See below, p. 162.

'6 or 12 hours', and said we might suppose 'as easily 20 months as 20 hours', which has become in the transcription, 'The limit allowed by the Greeks was 24 hours, but we might as well take 24 months.'[1]

The short-hand notes relate directly to the manuscript transcriptions in the brochures, not to the text of 1856. This is shown not merely by a rough conversion of a few pages into long-hand, which necessarily contains some guesswork, but by another kind of evidence. Many proper names, words in other languages than English, and some words for which the short-hand notation escaped him, were written out in long-hand by Collier as he was taking down his notes. These reveal a number of points where the short-hand notes and the brochures substantially agree, but the 1856 text is different. For instance, early in Lecture 9, Coleridge drew a brief comparison between Shakespeare and Calderon, saying 'he had been told that the Spanish poet Calderon had been as successful.' He had been told this, or rather had read it, in the copy of Schlegel's *Vorlesungen* presented to him shortly before he gave this lecture.[2] The name 'Calderon' is written out in the short-hand notes, and neither these, nor Schlegel, nor the transcript in the brochures mention 'Lopez de Vega' whose name is added in the 1856 text.[3] A little later Coleridge referred to the mirage-like effect known as the 'Fata Morgana' near Messina; in the short-hand notes the name is written out, with the first word spelt 'phata', as if Collier was not sure of it at the time. In the brochures a blank space is left for the name, which perhaps Collier did not understand, but in the 1856 text the reference to it has simply disappeared.[4] Then again, the name 'Catalani', which has also disappeared from the 1856 text, is represented as 'Cat¹'.[5] In Lecture 12 the short-hand notes coincide with the transcript in the brochures in reading 'poem called the Mad Mother', and the title is so written out, with initial capital letters, in the short-hand notes; in the 1856 text this is changed to 'In a modern poem a mad mother thus complains'.[6] Later in this lecture, Coleridge quoted a line from *Richard II*, noting it as a rare example of a name forming the whole line; this is written out in the short-hand notes as 'Harry Bolingbroke' [*sic*], and in the transcript in

---

1 For the context of these passages, see below, p. 101.

2 See below, p. 103 and n., and Raysor, II, 164 (126).

3 See below, p. 99 and n., and Raysor, II, 159 (122).

4 See below, p. 102 and n., where the text reads 'or as the [Fata Morgana] at Messina', and Raysor, II, 163 (125), where it is altered to 'In the same way, near Messina'.

5 See below, p. 103 and n., and Raysor, II, 164 (126).

6 See below, p. 119 and n., and Raysor, II, 185 (144).

the brochures appears as '*Harry* Bolingbroke', though Collier later inserted 'of' over the line, and also added in the margin 'Q Henry' (i.e. 'query Henry'?). 'Harry' is the form of the name as it appears in Isaac Reed's 1803 edition of Shakespeare, which Coleridge was using in this lecture, but in the 1856 text the name is changed to 'Henry'.[1]

These examples establish that in a number of crucial instances the short-hand notes and the manuscript brochures coincide, and differ from the 1856 text. All the evidence seems to confirm that the text in the brochures is based on the short-hand notes, that this text was transcribed at an early date, soon after the lectures were given, and is much closer to what Coleridge said than the 1856 text. A full new transcription of the short-hand notes would reveal some further differences between them and the text in the brochures, as at one point, for instance, the brochures and the 1856 text agree in reading 'Milton and Dante' as against 'Pindar and Dante' written out in the short-hand notes. However, there is good reason to think that the brochures provide a relatively polished text, worked up, probably with the help of memory, from the framework of notes Collier took at the lectures, but so soon afterwards as to guarantee a good degree of accuracy. That is to say, a full new transcription of the short-hand notes, if this could be made, would represent in a more or less curtailed and mangled form what survives in the manuscript brochures.

7

What, then, is to be said of the 1856 text, which is the text everyone knows from the reprints in Raysor's and other modern editions? It is clear that Collier lied when he said, 'In completing my transcripts . . . I have added no word or syllable of my own.'[2] It would be nearer the truth to say that he continually rewrote and added a great deal of material of his own. Almost every sentence is changed, most commonly by the addition of words or phrases that contribute little to the basic sense of the passage, as two examples will show. The first is from Lecture 9, where Coleridge was contrasting ancient drama with Shakespeare's. The passage is quoted first as it appears in the brochures, and then from the 1856 text as reprinted by Raysor:[3]

    (a) This had led Coleridge to consider that the ancient drama, meaning the works of Æschylus, Euripides, and Sophocles (for

---

[1] See below, p. 123 and n., and Raysor, II, 190 (148–9).

[2] *Seven Lectures*, Preface, vi–vii.

[3] See below, p. 99, and Raysor, II, 159 (122).

4 Page 2 from Collier's short-hand notes on Lecture 9 (for the printed text, see p. 162). On the facing page is a statement that this notebook was entered in court by Collier in support of an affidavit in January 1856 (see p. 158).

5 Page 3 from Collier's short-hand notes of Lecture 9 (for the printed text, see pp. 162-3). The facing page is blank.

the miserable rhetorical works by the Romans are scarcely to be mentioned as dramatic poems) might be contrasted with the Shakespearian Drama: he had called it Shakespearian, because he knew no other writer who had realized the same idea, although he had been told that the Spanish poet Calderon had been as successful.

(b) I have thus been led to consider, that the ancient drama (meaning the works of Æschylus, Euripides and Sophocles; for the rhetorical productions *of the same class* by the Romans are scarcely to be treated as *original* theatrical poems) might be contrasted with the Shakespearian drama.—I call it the Shakespearian drama *to distinguish it* because I know of no other writer who has realized the same idea, although I am told *by some*, that the Spanish poets, *Lopez de Vega and* Calderon, have been equally successful.

I have italicized words and phrases in the later version that could be omitted without changing the sense (the name 'Lopez de Vega' is not in Coleridge's source here, Schlegel, or in the short-hand notes). The other variants are of a typical kind too, like the omission of Coleridge's 'miserable', the one word that gives colour to a neutral passage, and the replacement of 'works' by 'productions', avoiding a repetition, but replacing a short word by a long one. All the way through the lectures small additions and expansions occur in the 1856 text that can be cut without loss. Often these are phrases qualifying a plain statement or a challenging comment by Coleridge, weakening it by 'as it were', 'sometimes', 'in many cases', 'generally', 'may be said to', or something of this kind. Collier was also fond of duplicating words so that 'attribute' in the brochure becomes 'trace and attribute'; 'with especial pleasure' is altered to 'with peculiar pleasure and satisfaction'; 'an age of high moral feeling' becomes 'an age of high moral feeling and lofty principle', and 'England overflowed' is changed to 'England may be said to have then overflowed'.[1]

However, such expansions could also seriously distort the sense, as a second example, from Lecture 6, may illustrate:[2]

(a) While he [i.e. Shakespeare] had the powers of a man, and more than man, yet he had all the feelings and manners which he painted in an affectionate young woman of 18.

[1] These examples all occur early in Lecture 6; see below, pp. 66–7, and Raysor, II, 114–16 (83–4).

[2] See below, p. 68, and Raysor, II, 119 (86).

(b) While Shakespeare possessed all the powers of a man, and more than a man, yet he had all the feelings, the sensibility, the purity, innocence and delicacy of an affectionate girl of eighteen.

By adding 'sensibility, the purity, innocence and delicacy', Collier has reduced a fine comment by Coleridge to something like sentimentality; Coleridge was not so seduced by rhetoric as to claim 'purity' or 'innocence' for Shakespeare. Again, Brae's charge that the 'vivid and peculiar phraseology' of Coleridge is not to be found in the 1856 text seems largely justified. Apart from the evidence already presented to show that this text is not closely related to the short-hand notebooks, it would appear most unlikely that, when Collier reconstructed a text for *Seven Lectures on Shakespeare and Milton*, he was able to recall much of what Coleridge had said forty-five years previously. It may well be that he could no longer even read his own short-hand notes with any certainty, for these too were old, and he had given up his work as a reporter years previously. In any case, it is clear that he dressed up the text he published in 1856 in his own style, and that it is in consequence unreliable and frequently misleading.

Some changes of a single word affect the sense radically, as, in Coleridge's description of Ariel, 'moral' in the brochures is changed to 'mortal' in the 1856 text: in the early text, Shakespeare, it is said, 'divests him of all moral character', and in the 1856 text this has become 'divests him of all mortal character'.[1] Collier's alterations are not neutral; they frequently alter the sense in subtle ways, and sometimes drastically. He also made a number of substantial additions and expansions. Some of these, like the elaboration of Coleridge's remarks on reading in a 'tone' early in Lecture 6,[2] or the addition of a passage referring to Spenser's *Faerie Queene* in Lecture 8,[3] may have been simply invented by Collier, for they do not materially contribute to the sense. It could be, however, that Collier was incorporating bits and pieces he recollected, or had noted elsewhere from Coleridge's conversation, or when he attended

[1] See below, p. 111, and Raysor, II, 176 (136).
[2] See below, p. 65, and Raysor, II, 112–13 (81). The passage beginning 'There may be a wrong tone' and ending 'of saying something that is worth hearing' was added in the 1856 text.
[3] See below, p. 93, and Raysor, II, 152 (115). Here, in order to introduce a familiar quotation from the end of *The Faerie Queene*, Bk. II, on Gryll's 'hoggish mind', Collier changed 'the sow in her sty', the phrase in the brochures, to 'the hog in the mire'. It is curious that the passage referred to in the previous note as an addition, and this one, both contain references to Spenser.

later lectures. There is no way of knowing for certain just how authentic any of the additions are, but the longer additions seem to be of the same kind as most of the shorter ones, elaborating, perhaps with an extra illustrative example like the quotation from Spenser, rather than materially extending what Coleridge said; they do not throw up any fresh ideas.

Collier's alterations in 1856 were not all additions and expansions. He made a number of cuts, removing proper names he did not see as relevant, or references he perhaps could not trace, like 'Catalani', 'Drummond', 'Monk Lewis', and 'Fata Morgana'.[1] He also left out, for no clear reason, some phrases that help to explain Coleridge's thinking; so, for example, in Lecture 7, Coleridge described Mercutio, according to the brochures, as 'a man possessing all the elements of a Poet: high fancy; rapid thoughts; the whole world was, as it were, subject to his law of association'. In the 1856 text the words 'high fancy; rapid thoughts' were omitted, a phrase which makes Coleridge's meaning more precise.[2] A more substantial instance occurs in Lecture 8, where Coleridge was commenting on Romeo; the passage is cited first as it appears in manuscript, and then as printed in 1856, from Raysor's text:[3]

(a) Such is frequently the case in the friendships of men of genius, and still more frequently in the first loves of ardent feelings and strong imaginations; *but still, for a man, having had the experience, without any inward feeling demonstrating the difference, to change one object for another seems without example.* But it is perfectly accordant with life.

(b) What is true of friendship is true of love, with a person of ardent feelings and warm imagination. What took place in the mind of Romeo was merely natural; it is accordant with every day's experience.

Here the passage italicized, which is omitted in the 1856 text, helps to make clear the drift of Coleridge's argument, by identifying what especially concerns him about Romeo, namely, how he could so suddenly change the object of his affections 'without any inward feeling demonstrating the difference', as if Rosaline and Juliet were the same.

The two most substantial passages occurring in the brochures but

---

[1] See below, respectively, pp. 103, 68, 73, 102, and Raysor II, 164 (126), 119 (86), 126 (93), 163 (125).

[2] See below, p. 78, and Raysor, II, 132 (98).

[3] See below, p. 97, and Raysor, II, 157 (119).

omitted from the 1856 text are both in Lecture 8. In the brochures the transcript of this lecture is marked as 'not finished', and it breaks off in the middle of a paragraph on the subject of taste; this is not included in the 1856 text.[1] Earlier in the same lecture Coleridge quoted two passages from Hooker's *Laws of Ecclesiastical Polity*, and commented on them. The passages are reproduced in a garbled form in the manuscript, as Collier seems to have been unable to take them down completely in short-hand, and evidently did not look them up to correct them. These are left out of the 1856 text, but Collier there added a curious footnote, stating that Coleridge quoted from Hooker, but that his record 'contains only a hint regarding it', and he could find 'no trace' of the exact words, or of a reference to them.[2] Possibly Collier noticed that the quotations from Hooker made little sense as he had noted them down, could not trace them readily and so decided simply to omit the whole paragraph in which they appear in the manuscript.

8

What Collier printed in 1856 in *Seven Lectures on Shakespeare and Milton* was a radically reconstructed version of some parts of his Diary and of the lectures Coleridge gave in 1811–12. He said he was adding nothing of his own, but in fact he altered both the Diary and the lecture notes freely. The original text of the Diary survives in the manuscript brochures now in the Folger Library, and these also contain early transcriptions of the short-hand notes Collier took at seven of the lectures Coleridge gave. These transcriptions are without doubt much closer than the 1856 text to what Coleridge said. It is not to be supposed that they represent exactly the words of his lectures; indeed, the varying lengths of the records Collier made of each lecture tend to support the comments he made, when he said that the notes were 'full of omissions, owing in some degree to want of facility on my part', and further that he was often 'so engrossed, and absorbed by the almost inspired look and manner of the speaker' as to be incapable of 'performing the mechanical duty of writing'.[3] However, they furnish a text that includes much of what Coleridge said in his words, and one that is substantially faithful to the spirit of his lectures. Two short-hand notebooks also survive, for Lectures 9 and 12, which clearly provided the copy from which these

---

[1] See below, p. 97, and Raysor, II, 157 (120).
[2] See below, p. 90, and Raysor, II, 150 (113).
[3] *Seven Lectures*, Preface, xiii.

lectures as given in the brochures were transcribed, and somewhat polished in the transcription. I have deciphered large sections of these notes, which reveal some differences in detail from the long-hand transcriptions. At best the short-hand notes provide a rough and abbreviated basis for these, but since they have an interest of their own, I have provided in Appendix C some more detailed comments, and I have printed there for comparison a substantial passage in three versions, as it was taken down in short-hand, as it was written out in long-hand, and as it was printed in *Seven Lectures on Shakespeare and Milton*. The material in this Appendix confirms that the long-hand transcriptions offer the best text available of Coleridge's lectures of 1811–12.

This text is printed in the following pages for the first time. The text Collier published in 1856 is readily available in the edition of T. M. Raysor, so that the interested reader will have no difficulty in comparing the two texts, should he wish to do so. The lectures are preceded by all those parts of the diary which relate to Coleridge. The text of this was much changed by Collier in 1856, when he also added substantial passages derived from elsewhere, perhaps from other notations of conversations with Coleridge. As Raysor reprinted only a few extracts in the Everyman edition of *Coleridge's Shakespearean Criticism* in 1960, and as both Collier's *Seven Lectures* and the first edition of Raysor are out of print and difficult to find, I have reprinted in Appendix A all the material relating to Coleridge that Collier included in his preface and claimed to be quoting from his Diary. I have added some notes in an attempt to help the reader by identifying proper names and quotations as far as possible, and by commenting on some points of special interest in relation to Raysor's edition. In the notes on Lectures 9 and 12, I have also commented on Coleridge's use of Schlegel, because I think Raysor is a little misleading on this matter. He refers his readers to the *Collected Works* of Schlegel, not to his lectures as Coleridge saw them, in a slightly different text, and quite differently divided, in the *Vorlesungen* published in 1809–11.[1]

---

[1] See below, p. 103, and n. Vol. II, Part 2, published in 1811, contained Schlegel's Lecture 12, on Shakespeare, which was subsequently revised, and published in his *Werke* divided into four lectures (it appears there as Lectures 23, 24, 25 and 26). Schlegel wrote a note in the 1811 volume explaining that the lectures as printed had been greatly enlarged, and added, 'The parts respecting Shakespeare and the English Theatre, in particular, have been almost altogether re-written' (Black, I, xii; *Vorlesungen*, II, ii, vii). Coleridge saw Schlegel's volume for the first time just before he delivered his own ninth lecture.

Notes on the presentation of the Text

Collier's long-hand manuscripts are very lightly pointed, and some passages have no punctuation at all. He often used a dash for a period, and a number of these have been retained. I have added enough punctuation to make the Diary and lecture notes easily readable. Collier frequently, but not invariably, used contractions for some common words, like the ampersand for 'and', and 'w^{ch}' for 'which'; I have silently expanded all of these. Occasionally he repeated a word, and all such duplications have been omitted. At other times he inadvertently left a word out, or wrote half a word at the end of a line, and omitted to complete it at the beginning of the next. In such cases I have supplied a word, or completed one, but all such additions are enclosed in square brackets.

Collier also made a number of corrections in the manuscript, and added some interlineations. These are of various kinds. Sometimes he mis-spelt a word, deleted it and started again. He also occasionally made a false start or misinterpreted his short-hand, as in Lecture 9[1] he wrote 'which', then deleted it and substituted 'while', clearly the correct word. In a similar way a little later he deleted 'predominant' and substituted 'prominent', and replaced 'intensely' by 'intentionally'. In all such cases I have simply printed Collier's final version, as I have done also in other instances where he substituted alternative words for those he first wrote. These may represent revisions as he went along, or changes made later, but in any case do not seriously affect the text. In some instances, Collier was striving for clarity, as when he replaced 'his' by 'Shakespeare's' (p. 75), and 'them' by 'the servants' (p. 77). More often there is no obvious reason for substitutions which appear to be rough equivalents for the word deleted. Examples are 'right' substituted for 'just' (p. 50); 'immediate pleasure' for 'positive pleasure' (p. 54); 'apt' for 'wont' (p. 55); 'justness' for 'propriety' (p. 57); 'thoughts' for 'ideas' (p. 65); 'Portrait' for 'painting' (p. 79); 'the aged' for 'old age' (p. 79); 'works' for 'writings' (p. 80); 'filial' for 'brotherly' (p. 85); 'term' for 'word' (p. 89); 'wonderful' for 'admirable' (p. 113); 'chasm' for 'blank' (p. 114); 'ceaseless' for 'perpetual' (p. 124); 'such as' for 'those who' (p. 124); 'mere fancy' for 'notion of mine' (p. 125); 'sentiment' for 'determination' (p. 127); 'new task' for 'action' (p. 128); 'irresolution' for 'inaction' (p. 128). These examples illustrate the extent to which such substitutions occur throughout the text of the lectures, and I have listed the most interesting ones.

---

[1] See below, p. 98.

One or two points of particular interest occur in Lecture 12, where Collier seems to have resumed transcribing after an interval of time. Here in one sentence he wrote 'sight', deleted this in favour of 'organs of vision', and then crossed out 'of vision' leaving merely 'organs' as the final text (p. 124). At another point part of a sentence is deleted, and nothing substituted: it occurs on p. 125, after the phrase 'Shakespeare himself', and runs as follows: 'as among other instances in Hamlet, not long after the Players come in, where he speaks of a drama "well digested in the scene, and set down with as much modesty as cunning" '. The manuscript also has one or two insignificant notes in pencil, besides the reference to 'short-hand note A' in Lecture 12. In Lecture 1 there is a pencilled note in the margin opposite a quotation from Jeremy Taylor referring to 'The Friend' (see p. 46), but no reference is made to this passage in Coleridge's *The Friend*. A few other difficulties are remarked in the notes below.

The entries relating to Coleridge in John Payne Collier's diary, October–November 1811

Sunday October 13th

I mentioned a few pages ago being in company with Godwin and not hearing him say a single good thing—A few months ago I was in Coleridge's Company several times and was highly delighted with a fund of anecdote and humour, much good nature and correct observation, besides a vast extent of knowledge delivered with much eloquence. He gave the following character of Falstaff, which I set down soon after he had delivered it. It was given in conversation at my Father's House, December 23rd 1810[1]—

'That Falstaff was no Coward but pretended to be one merely for the sake of trying experiments on mankind!! That he was a liar only with the same object and not because he loved falsehood for itself! That he was a man of such pre-eminent abilities that he had a profound contempt for all those around him, and was determined to make them, notwithstanding their fancied superiority, his absolute tools. He knew that however low he degraded himself his own talents would extricate him from every difficulty. When he was conceived to be the greatest rogue, thief, and liar he still had that about him which rendered him, or which could render him, not only respectable but absolutely necessary. It was in characters of complete moral depravity and yet of excellent wit and first rate talents that Shakespeare delighted, such as Richard III, Iago, Falstaff, etc.'

Coleridge is a man very fond of the display of his abilities, and perhaps very naturally and I am sure very usefully so—for no one can

---

[1] *December 23rd 1810*] This date is omitted from the 1856 Preface.

hear him speak if he be ever such a dolt but must improve by what he says. After supper on the night when he said what I have related of Falstaff he was most entertaining indeed. No one spoke but he, and no one wished to speak, indeed he kept us on the continual listen and laugh so that it was almost impossible.

Thursday October 17th

Yesterday evening at C. Lamb's I met S. T. Coleridge, of whom I have made previous mention. I had previously made up my mind that if I saw him I would set down on the tablet of my memory everything that he said worthy of recollection. I went into the room where he and many more were at $\frac{1}{2}$ past 8, and before a quarter past 9 my mind was so burdened with the things worthy of recollection that he said that I was obliged to relieve myself by quitting his company, and not attending to him for the remainder of the night. When I returned, however, do all I could, I found it impossible to keep my attention off him: it is as impossible for a man that can see to avoid being sensible that the sun shines on a clear mid-summer day as it is to be in company with Coleridge and not to attend to him. The following, as well as Memory serves me, is the substance, and the mere substance, of what he said, though I fear that I shall fall short of giving even the substance of what he expressed with a *before unknown felicity of language*.

In speaking of Shakespeare, on whom he was conversing when I entered the room, he said that he was almost the only dramatic poet who, by the characters he drew, represented a class and not an individual: that other poets, and in other respects good ones too, had always aimed their satire at individual and particular foibles, while Shakespeare at one stroke lashed thousands. He drew a parallel between Shakespeare and the geometrician, which I was not able fully to comprehend, but the object of which was to shew that, though in forming a circle the eye was fixed upon the centre as the important point, yet that it always included a wide circumference. So in Shakespeare, while the eye was riveted upon the individual character introduced, that character always included a circle of others, which inclusion did not at all diminish the interest for the particular person portrayed—Othello he mentioned as an instance of this kind.

From Shakespeare he went on to Beaumont and Fletcher, of whose Comedies he spoke in terms of high commendation, but to whose tragedies he felt great objections. Their tragedies always proceeded upon something unnatural and forced: the reader or auditor could never reconcile it with probability, and sometimes not even with possibility. For instance, one of their Tragedies[1] proceeded upon this point: A lady had expressed her wish to *possess the heart of her Lover*, which the Lover had understood all the way through in a literal sense, and nothing would satisfy him but that he must tear out his heart and present it to her, in order to secure her affections when he should be past the enjoyment of them.—Their comedies, however, were of a much superior cast, and rivalled in some instances Shakespeare.

The Tragedies of Beaumont and Fletcher brought to his mind those of Kotzebue, the celebrated German Playwright, whose pieces were of a similar cast to those of the United authors. His tragedies always strained the imagination beyond what it was possible for it to bear. Kotzebue in his mind was, even in the line where he was supposed to excel, viz. Tragedy, worse than Beaumont and Fletcher, and did not possess a grain of their comic wit and talent.

From thence he went on to speak of the Gamester,[2] written I think by Moore. The situations he admitted were frequently very affecting, but in the language of the piece there was nothing that was valuable. It was extremely natural for anyone to cry at seeing a beautiful woman in the depths of anguish and despair at seeing her husband, who had ruined himself by gaming, poisoned at the very moment he had come into a large fortune, and might have lived in affluence and happiness; but there was nothing in it to improve the heart, or enlighten the understanding. To be sure it produced tears, and so would a blunt razor on shaving the upper lip.

The Curse of Kehama[3] was then introduced by one of the Company. Coleridge stated it to be a poem of much talent, ingenuity, and imagination, and which did the highest credit to its author; but there were two things in it completely incompatible; from the wildness of the story it was absolutely necessary that the Reader should fancy himself enjoying one of the wildest dreams that visit the poet's fancy, and at the same time it was required (which was utterly impossible) that the soul should be alive to all the feelings of social tenderness: The Reader was required to believe in the possibility of the existence of an almighty man, completely detestable for his crimes, who had extorted from heaven the power he possessed by mere prayers; and yet to be sensible to the delicate affec-

---

[1] *Tragedies*] The tragedy referred to here is *The Mad Lover* (so Collier). With these general remarks on Beaumont and Fletcher, cf. below, p. 74.

[2] *Gamester*] A tragedy by Edward Moore, staged in 1753. It had some celebrity, and is mentioned by Wordsworth in his Preface to *Lyrical Ballads*.

[3] *The Curse of Kehama*] Southey's poem was published in 1810.

tions of parent and child oppressed, injured, insulted, and punished. This was incompatible with human nature. The design of the poem was excellent, viz. to shew the superiority of moral to physical power. He thought it a work of great talent but not so much genius, and he drew the distinction between talent and genius that there is between a Watch and an Eye: each were beautiful in their way, but the one was made the other grew. Talent was a manufactured thing: genius was born. It was suggested by one of the Company that more credit was given to Southey for imagination in that poem than was due to him, because persons in general were not acquainted with the Indian Mythology, and thought that fancy which was in truth only derived from the extravagances of Indian Mythology. Coleridge replied to this that the story was Southey's, and indeed the mythology was greatly his: he had invented the story, and wanted to reconcile it with possibility according to some theory, and therefore resorted to eastern fiction: he had picked up this mythology from books by scraps, and had tacked them together according as his imagination or wishes dictated.

Another of the persons present noticed Walter Scott's Poems. Coleridge professed himself almost completely ignorant of them, and therefore was not competent to form a judgment. He had had the Lady of the Lake[1] by him some months, but had only read the two first books, in which he had found at least two hundred grammatical blunders: that were not English on this side the Tweed, nor indeed on the other, for they had none. If it were necessary for him to form an opinion of Mr. Scott and his poems, the first thing he would do would be to take away all his names of old castles which rhimed very prettily and seemed very picturesque: next he would remove from the poem all the names of old armour: then he would exclude all names of old nunneries, Abbies, and priories, and then he would see what remained. Of this at present he could be no competent judge from his having read so little. There would then remain: the fable or story on which it was founded (for the selection of which he gave him full credit), the imagination, and the felicity of expression. Of these others must judge.

I should have noticed that after Shakespeare notice was made of Milton's *Samson Agonistes*, which Coleridge said was formed on the model of the Ancients. One of the Company observed that Stephens[2] (Shakespeare's Commentator) said that it was formed on the model of

---

[1] *The Lady of the Lake*] Scott's poem was published in May 1810.
[2] *Stephens*] George Steevens, best known for his edition of Shakespeare in 1773, revised in 1778.

the Ancient Mysteries, the origin of the Drama. Coleridge flew at this, asserting that Stephens was no more able to understand the beauties of Milton or Shakespeare than he was to form an idea of the grandeur and glory of the Seventh Heavens. He would require more than a Herchellean Telescope[1] of 10 feet diameter for him to see half a quarter as far.

In allusion to Scott, I think, Coleridge mentioned a beautiful figure in Burns,[2] which he said was worth three times as much as his country-man had or ever would write

> Like snow that falls upon a River
> A moment white then gone for ever—

This was said by Burns in allusion to the transitoryness of pleasure.

As an instance of strong description Coleridge quoted the following from a German Poet,[3] a Blacksmith: 'I saw an old woman bent double with age warming herself piecemeal[4] limb by limb over a scanty pot of fire.'

The above is all I recollect that he said upon literary subjects; on Political matters he talked little excepting on the state of Ireland, on which he observed that Ireland was far behind us in civilization, and that we had attempted most absurdly to effect her complete civilization merely by the operation of an act of Parliament. It had now been five centuries conquered (Henry 2nd), and yet the lower classes were in absolute barbarism: even in the Capital of the Island they talked a jargon more savage than in the wilds of the new world. We ought to have acted towards Ireland as the Romans did towards Spain, which could not be said to be completely subdued until the middle of the reign of Augustus. They planted garrisons in different parts of the Country, and when any of the natives distinguished themselves for talents, industry, or bravery, he was rewarded as he deserved, and promoted to the rights of a Citizen, so that almost within 50 years after the conquest of it Spaniards were seen sitting as Senators at Rome. How different was the conduct of England to Ireland: where the people were deprived of all privileges, and no talents were encouraged because the nation happened

---

[1] *Herchellean telescope*] Alluding to Sir William Herschel (1738–1822), who greatly developed the telescope for astronomical study.

[2] *Burns*] Inaccurately citing ll. 61–2 from *Tam O'Shanter*. This was a favourite quotation of Coleridge's; see, for example, *The Friend*, ed. Barbara Rooke (1969), I, 110.

[3] *German poet*] untraced.

[4] *Piecemeal*] Collier wrote 'peacemeal'.

to be papists: they were papists too of the lowest description, with all its superstition, and without any of its impressiveness, grandeur, and sublimity. Neither in Italy, Spain, nor France were they now papists.

It had been said as a matter of boast that all our best officers were Scotsmen and our best soldiers Irishmen. It might be true, but this did not include the inference that Englishmen would not make good soldiers. The truth was that the reason Englishmen did not go into the army as much as Scotsmen or Irishmen was because they had something better to do. It was only the beggarly nobility of Scotland that sent their younger sons into the army, because they were too proud to put them into trade, and that was the reason there were so many Scots officers: Wherever there were most idle raggamuffins and blackguards there would be most soldiers obtained, and the greater part of the army was composed of such blackguards. Was there a man who had a dread of execution? He went into the army to be shot instead of being hanged. In a family, if one of the sons was remarkably wild and extravagant and ungovernable, they made him a soldier. Was there another, a cold calculating steady disposition, he was a tradesman: and was there a third who had sufficient confidence, but remarkably stupid, he was sure to be a parson. There was no ability in Coleridge's opinion so questionable as military talent, because it required so little more than mere foolhardyhood. He was the best soldier who had most confidence in himself. So in boxing the late James Belcher,[1] who was originally a little blackguard playing in St. Paul's churchyard Bristol, by licking all the boys there, got such self-confidence that none could stand against him. He felt himself sure of victory, and it always happened, where this feeling prevailed, the person possessing it was sure to impress his antagonist with dread.— This was universally the case. It was this self-confidence that had led Buonaparte's arms to victory; and not, as had been supposed, consummate generalship. Coleridge did not think Buonaparte a man of very pre-eminent abilities.

I omitted to mention after the Curse of Kehama the praise Coleridge bestowed on the *Arabian Nights Entertainments*, as contradistinguished from that Poem. It was true that in reading them you were obliged to imagine yourself in a kind of dream in order to make some of the relations even possible, but the author (and this was his praise) never required you to be awakened by any touches of fine feeling or sentiment. Your sleep was undisturbed while your fancy was on the wing.

This as well as I can remember is the substance of the conversation.

---

[1] *James Belcher*] 'Jem' Belcher (1781–1811), the celebrated prizefighter.

Would that I could have imparted to it a twentieth part of the eloquence of Coleridge. It is impossible for a man to talk better.

Sunday October 20th

This day I again had the delight of being in company with the greatest man of the present day, and in some respects unrivalled in any former age. How humbling it is to the arrogance of youth to be in company with men of such transcendent abilities. I think I never felt my own insignificance so strongly: indeed, into whatever society he goes he must be, to use a common proverb, 'inter stellas luna minores'—His powers of conversation are surprising, arising from his extensive knowledge. Let the subject that is started be what it may, whether law, medicine or policy, he is as much prepared as if he had studied all his life: he seems to know by intuition, as it were, what it has cost common men lives to acquire. He is besides so clear-headed, but if in conversation he is contradicted or opposed he seldom pursues his point and maintains his position, which may be owing to his fear of giving offence, but more probably because he has not that thorough knowledge of the subject which would ensure success to his argument. He is one of the most profound metaphysicians in the world, and, as a warm advocate for Kant's German Philosophy, has a supreme contempt for Locke, whom he accuses of having adopted the Greek word Idea and misapplied it. Coleridge contends that it means only images of things that have not been the objects of sense, while Locke asserts that an idea is the result of a previous impression upon the organs. So at least I understood him, but my ignorance of Metaphysics will not allow me to be positive. Before Locke's time the word Idea was never misapplied as he has done. It was used by Pindar, Aristophanes, Aristotle, and Plato, who employed it in this way. You were walking—You saw something at a distance which you supposed to be a sheep; you could not see the head or the legs, but what you saw gave you the idea of a sheep. He dined with us, and from that time till supper his conversation was on Military punishments, Criminal Law; Sir Alexander Ball,[1] and our Conduct towards Sicily— He also introduced the following Epitaph which he had made upon the late Lord Lonsdale,[2] who, to use his own words, 'seemed to make him-

[1] *Sir Alexander Ball*] He died while Governor of Malta in 1809. Coleridge served under him there, admired him, and wrote an account of him, published in *The Friend*; see the edition by Barbara Rooke (1969), I, 532–80.
[2] *Lord Lonsdale*] Sir James Lowther, Earl of Lonsdale, known as the 'bad earl', who died in 1802. The troubles the Wordsworth family had with him over his

self happy by making everybody else unhappy'—

> A very old proverb commands that we should
> Relate of the dead only that which is good
> But of the great Earl who lies here on lead
> We know nothing good but—that he is dead.

It is now too late (1 o'clock in the morning) to proceed on this subject, but shall continue it in my diary tomorrow.

Monday October 21st

I this morning resume the subject of the Conversation of Coleridge.

At Dinner and after it (for I shall set down things as they occur to my mind without relation to the order exactly in which they were spoken) the conversation turned upon the French Medicine of L'eau Medicinale for the Gout, and Coleridge, who spoke upon it exactly as if he had been educated a Physician, gave us its rise and progress. It was first employed by a French Physician named Huson,[1] and as it was very violent in its consequences, the Police interfered and prohibited its use. For some time it was laid aside, but again brought forward in France, from whence it has been imported into England. Mr. Moore (brother to Mr. John Moore)[2] attempted to analyse it and found that it contained a great deal of White Hellebore and Opium, the latter not made with brandy but with a weak white wine. It is now manufactured of these ingredients in England.

After Dinner Coleridge gave us a few of his definitions as well as after supper: the first was the distinction between *Genius*, *Talent* and *Cleverness*. Of the two first he said something at Lamb's (for which see Thursday last) but the last he described to be a mere secondary mechanical quality. Thus, for instance, Davy[3] the Chemist would sometimes, reflecting with himself, make a new and important discovery but was at

refusal to pay his debts are recorded in Mary Moorman's *William Wordsworth: The Early Years*, 1770–1803 (1957), 167–9. The epitaph is not included in E. H. Coleridge's edition of Coleridge's *Poems*.

---

[1] *Huson*] Presumably Henri-Marie Husson, born 1772, a noted member of the faculty of medicine in Paris, and a specialist on vaccination, who published numerous medical treatises.

[2] *Mr. Moore (brother to Mr. John Moore)*] I cannot identify this 'Mr. Moore' with any certainty.

[3] *Davy*] Later Sir Humphry Davy; see below, p. 65, and n.

a loss to make himself intelligible by demonstrating his idea chemically. Upon this the under-chemist, who was what is called 'a clever fellow', would hit upon some expedient for explaining it. This was *cleverness*; it was the adaptation of means to ends.

His next remark was upon what, he observed, have been generally thought to be synonymous terms—*Fancy* and *Imagination*. He thought that there was a wide difference between them: to illustrate it by analogy —in his opinion *Fancy* might be considered delirium, and *Imagination* madness. The one a thing transient and not long continued, and the other a permanent feeling: the one warm, the other scorching. I confess for myself they may differ in degree, but according to his own account they do not differ in kind.

I adverted in my account dated yesterday to Coleridge's metaphysics. He gave the following opinion concerning Locke. 'That Locke's name had been always triumphantly united with that of Newton, and, as if Newton had overturned DesCartes' system of Physics, it was said of Locke that he had overthrown DesCartes' system of metaphysics.' In his opinion there was nothing more erronious than this assertion. DesCartes was far above Locke, as the sun is above a twinckling star, and he would venture to say that there was not a word that was new in all that the English metaphysician had said: not only had he taken hints from old books, but he had borrowed all the sentiments, and sometimes phrases, of their authors without any acknowledgement. In short, he lived in an age of little knowledge and less thought, for knowledge and thought went hand in hand, and had very happily applied the ignorance of the times to the ignorance of the times. Coleridge then introduced a remark,[1] which I think he borrowed from Dr. Johnson, that 'truths acknowledged and esteemed incontrovertible in one age are destroyed in another, and again raised up at a distant period to astonish mankind as a new discovery'—So it was with Locke; all he had done was to bring forward what had been said long before and forgotten, and to misapply the word *Idea* which he never comprehended. He did not believe that Locke was anything of a Greek scholar; on the contrary, in consulting Aristotle he had almost uniformly adopted the later translation without reference to the original: he gave as an instance [that] what in Aristotle had been translated as 'Ideæ innatæ' ought to have been construed 'Ideæ in-generatæ'; or as he would English it, 'Ideas begotten upon the senses'. I may be wrong in this because my ignorance of metaphysics is such as not perhaps to allow me to comprehend exactly the distinction. St.

---

[1] *remark*] I have not traced this quotation.

Matthew,[1] speaking of sights seen after the Resurrection, says that he beheld flames that gave *Ideas of faces*, using it in its correct sense exactly as the ancients had employed it.

Thus much he said of Locke; to Spinosa he paid high compliments, observing that, provided you admitted his first proposition[2] (which was certainly wrong), you might as well try to break an adamantyne chain with a rush as to deny or overturn any of his conclusions. I must endeavour to inform myself more about Spinosa before I mention his first proposition which is said to be so faulty. DesCartes is a great favourite with Coleridge, as I have, I believe, already said.

Upon the subject of the Deity Coleridge was peculiarly happy, at least so it struck me, but in relating what he said I am certain I shall so far fall short of the original as perhaps scarcely to make myself intelligible, where he was as clear as rock water, and as grateful. In religion Coleridge is completely an enthusiast, and maintains that it must be founded upon moral feeling, and not upon reason: it must be built on the passions, and not on the understandings of mankind. In his mind, the moment you began to reason, that moment you ceased to be religious. For this reason he denied that Unitarians had no religion: theirs was a theory: he had been brought up to the Church, and had left it for the unity of God: he was still a friend of the unity of the Creator, but he did not reason upon it: he could not do it: if any person asked him why he believed in the existence of a God, his answer was because he ought: but he would not attempt to prove the existence of God, as many did from his works: no: if he acknowledged a Creator, every feeling of his heart, every being in his works, were in harmony and vibrated with the notion: if he did not acknowledge a God, all was confusion and disorder. He therefore believed in God because he ought, and could give no other reason; nor would he seek for any.

Much conversation took place, as I believe I have noticed, upon the subject of military punishments, on which Coleridge warmly contended that flogging had a bad moral effect upon the men: it made them think meanly of themselves, than which nothing could be worse: It degraded them to a level with brutes, and when that is the case they will not

---

[1] *St. Matthew*] Coleridge was referring to Matthew, XXVIII, 3, where the Greek text runs: ἦν δὲ ἡ ἰδέα αὐτοῦ ὡς ἀστραπή. (Authorized version, 'His countenance was like lightning.')

[2] *first proposition*] In Spinoza's *Ethics*, the first proposition concerning God ('Substance is by nature prior to its modifications'), or the first proposition concerning the mind ('Thought is an attribute of God, or God is a thinking thing').

scruple to perform the action of Brutes, might be added. He related several instances of inhuman barbarity, on the part of officers to the men under them, with such feeling and eloquence as made one shudder. From military punishments he proceeded to the general administration of the criminal law of the land, and Robinson quoted here a Preface written by Emelyn[1] to the state trials, in which that lawyer said that the civil law was very defective and the criminal complete. From considering the law of England, Coleridge went on to compare it with other countries, particularly Italy, where it was so defective that men were obliged to take it into their own hands and this gave rise to the numerous assassinations. 'Right', said he, 'is right, and men will have it if it can be procured: the mind never rests satisfied under injustice, and when justice is done it is alone contented'. He quoted Lord Bacon who says in his Essay on Revenge that it is 'wild justice', and adds, 'which the more man's nature runs to, the more ought law to weed it'. A man feels himself injured, he finds no Judge that will give him redress, and he seeks it himself: his dagger is the instrument of Justice: the better therefore the law is administered, the less and less will revenge become a passion actuating the mind.

This naturally led to a discussion on the comparative benefits to be derived to Society from the law being to be procured at a dear or a cheap rate. Coleridge maintained the propriety of dear law because, in order that the Judges should be independent in mind, it was necessary that they should be independent in purse, when they had no temptation to take bribes because they did not want money. Robinson,[2] on the contrary, supported the necessity of having law cheap, that all might be able to purchase it: much may certainly be said on both sides, but the argument in favour of cheap law supposes that all men have not this right because it is dear; but supposing it were cheap, and the fees of Judges, Counsel, and officers were less than they are, more would resort to the Court for justice, so that if their emoluments were less they would be oftener receiving them, and, though they had more to do, they would in the end be as well paid; provided the fees were not too much reduced. At present there can be no doubt that many abuses prevail, and that, if

---

[1] *Emelyn*] Sollom Emlyn (1697–1754), who contributed a well-known preface to the State Trials (1730), reprinted in *Cobbett's Complete Collection of State Trials* (4 vols., 1809); see especially I, xxiv–xxv.

[2] *Robinson*] Henry Crabb Robinson gives a brief account of this occasion in his diary under the date 20 October 1811, but he does not record the conversation. See *Henry Crabb Robinson on Books and their Writers*, ed. Edith J. Morley (1938), 48–9.

they were remedied, and only those fees taken which are strictly due, law would be sold much cheaper than it now is obtained. Thus at least I think on the subject.

Coleridge was not particularly happy last night when he got on the subject of Poetry—he declared neither Southey, Scott, or Campbell to be Poets according to his definition: in his mind that man was a Poet who employed the most common occurrences in life to his purpose: who took advantage of what was seen every day and neglected, and brought it forward to ensure conviction: as a specimen of this he gave the lines I have before noticed, as quoted by him from Burns,[1]

> Like snow that falls upon a river
> A moment white then gone for ever,

where the image employed must have been seen daily, but never used or applied so happily. Shakespeare was full of these familiar images, and Milton, but the specimen he gave from the latter certainly did not very well exemplify what he was supporting: speaking of the advent of the Messiah, Milton says[2] that he advanced with thousands and ten thousands of angels in his train, and adds, 'far on his coming shone'. I do not know exactly where this passage is taken from, but certainly it is no very happy illustration of a familiar image: it is undoubtedly sublime thought to suppose the glory of his presence shoots so far before him, but ten thousand of these might be quoted. Coleridge adverted next to the principles on which Poets were to be tried: what was the true touchstone of talent, which was as I have stated above, before I quoted the lines from Burns. On being asked whether Southey, Scott, or Campbell would live, he prefaced his answer by disclaiming all envy, and by declaring that he would give according to his opinion a fair, candid, and true answer: as an honest man, he must say that he thought none of them would live beyond their day: their works had not the seeds of life within them. The two first were entertaining, and the first possessed talent, but he professed that he did not understand the latter. He was incomprehensible. All Poetry in his view should be capable of being reduced to prose, and that could not be poetry worth reading that was not intelligible in prose as well as verse: if this were true, Mr. Campbell was no poet. Southey was like an elegant setter of jewels, but the stones were supplied to him: he gave neatness and some beauty, but they gave the lustre to his works. He said little of Wordsworth, but from what did fall from him it was

---

[1] *Burns*] See above, p. 34.
[2] *Milton says*] In *Paradise Lost*, VI, 767, 'far off his coming shone'.

plain to be seen that he thought him a greater poet than any other living. He declared that he himself had no title to the name of Poet according to his definition. He had many years ago published a Volume of Poems; that is to say, they had been published for him. Cottle[1] of Bristol offered him £20 for some pieces he had written at College without the slightest idea of publication, and Coleridge took it: his poverty and not his will consented, and he was dubbed author before he knew where he was. He received but about £15 for them and then the Reviewers styled him a Poet, and fell foul of him for bombastic buckram in his language: 500 Copies were sold, and a second edition was published, in which Coleridge pleaded guilty to the charge of inflated language.[2] Since Wordsworth had printed his poems the Reviewers had again laid their talons upon him, and accused him of not only belonging to a School, but of being the head of a School employing and affecting *mock simplicity*[3] of expression, thus directly contradicting their former assertion that he had employed nothing in the formation of his poems but *bombastic buckram*. Since that time he had published no poems excepting two not with his name in Wordsworth's volumes.

We suffered last night a severe loss indeed, as his memory would not serve him to repeat two of his Poems, one called the 'Walk of the Devil',[4] being a satyrical short effusion in which he was assisted by Southey, according to his own account; it represented the Devil coming from his dwelling in hell to visit his 'snug little farm on the earth' to 'see how his stock went on', in which he proceeds through the various professions and occupations of life, shewing their vices, and the satisfaction the Devil felt in seeing his stock thrive so well. I am able to say this much of it

---

[1] *Cottle*] Joseph Cottle advanced thirty guineas to Coleridge for *Poems on Various Subjects* (1796); a second edition appeared in 1797.

[2] *inflated language*] *Poems by S. T. Coleridge*, Second Edition, 1797, has an additional preface in which Coleridge wrote, 'My poems have been rightly charged with a profusion of double-epithets and a general turgidness.'

[3] *mock simplicity*] Alluding probably to Jeffrey's notorious review of Southey's *Thalaba* in *The Edinburgh Review*, II, (1802), 63ff., in which Wordsworth and Coleridge's *Lyrical Ballads* are attacked especially for their 'affectation of great simplicity', and 'perverted taste for simplicity'.

[4] *Walk of the Devil*] Printed in *The Morning Post*, 6 September 1799, as 'The Devil's Thoughts', a poem in fourteen stanzas, including the two inaccurately cited here as Stanzas 4 and 3 respectively. It was reprinted in Coleridge's *Poetical Works* (1828), and was later expanded to fifty-seven stanzas by Southey, who published it as 'The Devil's Walk' in 1838. The poem had some celebrity, and it must have been widely known under this title, since it was imitated by Shelley in his 'The Devil's Walk' (1812), and by Byron in 'The Devil's Drive' (1813).

because I have before heard it read. I think I remember two of the verses.

> He saw a 'Pothecary on a white horse
> Riding forth on his vocations,
> And the Devil was pleased, for it put him in mind
> Of *Death* in the Revelations.

> He saw a Lawyer killing a serpent
> On a Dunghill behind a stable,
> And the Devil laughed, for it put him in mind
> Of the story of Cain [and] *Abel*.

The keen satyre of these two verses cannot but be felt by everyone, in the first making Death and the Apothecary almost synonimous, and in the last describing the innocent Abel as a serpent, and the lawyer as the wicked Cain—thereby insinuating that the wily serpent was an angel compared with the lawyer.

Coleridge told us (though I fancy from his indecision of character it will turn out to be nothing more than a tale) that it was his intention to give lectures at Coachmakers' Hall[1] on Poetry, with the view of erecting some standard under which all true Poets might be ranged. This would, he observed, be his main object but he should also introduce various criticisms on Shakespeare and Milton, to whom he should devote several of the Lectures. Such a thing was, in his opinion, very much wanted, and he should put it in execution, he said, next month, if he could procure a sufficient number of subscribers. What makes me doubt of this plan being put into effect is that, although he spoke so positively of delivering them at Coachmakers' Hall, he did not even know where it was!

Last year[2] he delivered Lectures upon Poetry at the Royal Institution,

---

[1] *Coachmakers' Hall*] Henry Crabb Robinson's note in his diary for 30 October 1811 (*Henry Crabb Robinson on Books and their Writers*, I, 49–50), stating that Coleridge showed him a prospectus of a course of lectures that day, tends to confirm Collier's story. Robinson says it offered subscriptions for a lady at two guineas, 'a gentleman three guineas, with power to bring a lady four guineas'. The surviving prospectus for the lectures of 1811–12 (see above, p. viii) offers single tickets at two guineas, 'or 3 guineas with the privilege of introducing a lady', and announces that they are to be given in 'Scot's Corporation Hall'. Coleridge sent a prospectus, presumably this later one, to Robinson in a letter of 8 November 1811 (*Collected Letters*, III, 339–40, 343). If an earlier prospectus was drafted or printed, no copy survives.

[2] *Last year*] Collier possibly misunderstood Coleridge, who must have been referring to the lectures he gave at the Royal Institution in 1808. There is no other evidence that Coleridge gave lectures anywhere in 1810.

and he said that for the first lecture he prepared himself and when it was finished he received many high flown but frigid compliments, which had evidently been before studied. For the next Lecture he prepared himself less, and was much admired; for the third Lecture, and for the remainder, he did not prepare himself at all, and was most enthusiastically applauded and approved, and the Theatre completely filled. The reason was in his mind obvious, for what he said came warm from the heart and, as my father justly added, what came warm from the heart of the speaker went warm to the heart of the hearer; and Coleridge subjoined that although the observations might not be so remarkably good or so well illustrated, yet being illustrated at the moment by objects before the eyes of the auditors, they felt and acknowledged them.

I have mentioned before the sentiment of Dr. Johnson[1] regarding the fluctuation of public opinion, viz. (I use his own words) 'The opinions prevalent in one age as truth beyond the reach of controversy are refuted and rejected in another, and rise again to reception in remoter times'. This sentiment Coleridge beautifully illustrated classically, by referring to Virgil,[2] who represents certain spirits, [which] after [having] been steeped for some time in the oblivious waters of Lethe, rise again to life and activity.

---

[1] *Dr. Johnson*] See above, p. 38 and n.
[2] *Virgil*] See *Aeneid*, VII, 739–51.

3

Collier's diary: the transcripts of Lectures 1 and 2

This afternoon Coleridge delivered his first lecture. It was occupied by explaining the causes of false criticism. As any observation of mine would be superfluous and idle, I shall merely insert the notes I took of the Lecture.

He commenced, as might be expected, with alluding to the difficulty of a task which, however, he had voluntarily undertaken; a difficulty arising not less from his own deficiency than from the wide extent of his subject: 'inopem me copia facit'[1]—He trusted as he proceeded he should by his manner of treating the subject induce the sympathy of his hearers which, like the sun, the Spring, or the Showers, were absolutely necessary to produce the promised fruits. He adverted to his own life which had been spent more in reading and conversation than in publishing, for he had never felt the desire, so often experienced by others, of becoming an author. He had other obstacles to overcome lest he should wound the pride of conscious superiority or excite contempt, the worst— and most absurd—passion that could actuate a human and intellectual being.

On the first examination of a work it would be right to observe to what feeling or passion of the human mind it addresses itself—whether to the benevolent, the vindictive, or to others, or to *Envy or its common mask Scorn*, and to inquire in the next place whether the pleasure we receive from it had a tendency to keep us good, to make us better, or to reward us for being good.

---

[1] *inopem me copia facit*] 'wealth makes me poor'; a tag Coleridge liked to use; see for example, *Letters*, III, 126.

He went on to notice the causes of false criticism, especially in poetry (but not confining it to that only), during which it would be necessary for him to represent the obstacles that interrupted the formation of a sane judgment. These were either

1. Accidental, arising from the particular circumstances of the age in which we live, or

2. Permanent, flowing from the general principles of our nature.

Under the first head, *accidental causes*, might be classed 1. the events that had occurred during our own day, which had themselves from their importance created a world of readers; 2. the practice of public speaking, which encouraged a too great desire to be understood at the first blush; 3. the prevalence of Reviews, Magazines, Novels, newspapers, etc.

In allusion to reading novels, he said that it was such a distraction of the mind, such an utter loss to the reader, that he could not so well call it *passtime* as *killtime*. It was filling the mind with a little mawkish sensibility instead of encouraging and cultivating the more noble faculties.

Reviews were pernicious because the writers decided without any reference to fixed principles, because they were filled with personalities, and above all because they taught people rather to judge than to read: they encouraged superficiality, and a disposition to adopt the sentiments dictated under the word *WE*, [rather] than to form opinions of our own. In Elder Time writers were looked up to as intermediate beings between Angels and men. Some time afterwards they were thought venerable teachers; from thence they descended to instructive friends, and now they were deemed rather culprits than benefactors, and the first question asked of a person who was reading generally was, 'What trash have you there?' There was some reason for this difference, he allowed, for in these times if a man had failed as a shoe-maker and could read and write, *for spelling was not necessary*, he became author.

Coleridge here quoted from Bishop Jeremy Taylor[1] who, he observed, though writing in prose, might be considered one of the first of our Poets. The passage related to the subject he was discussing, and contained among others the following sentence.

---

[1] *Taylor*] Coleridge misquotes a sentence from the dedicatory letter to Lord Hatton (Sig. AI^r) in *ΣΥΜΒΟΛΟΝ ΘΕΟΛΟΓΙΚΟΝ or a Collection of Polemicall Discourses* (1674); the text should read, 'and the breath of the people is like the voice of an exterminating Angel, not so killing but so secret; but that's not all; it is also as contingent as the smiles of an infant, or the fall of a die.' In the 1856 text the quotation is omitted, and Collier merely records in a footnote that Coleridge quoted from an unidentified work by Jeremy Taylor (Raysor, II, 58 (34)).

'The favour of the people is as fickle as the smiles of children or the fall of a die.'

After censuring personality, Coleridge quoted from (I believe) the Lectures he had himself formerly delivered at the Royal Institution, in which he contended that the present was 'an age of personality and political gossip', where insects, as in Ægypt, were worshipped and valued in proportion to the venom of their sting—Where Poems, particularly satyres, were valued in proportion to the number of living names they contained, and where 'the notes had this comparative merit, that they were generally more poetical than the text'. This was one of the principal supports of the 'Scotch professorial Court'.[1] He had once seen an Epic Poem advertized with this recommendation subjoined, 'that it contained more than 100 names of living characters'.[2]

The Lecturer delivered one of the [most] beautiful passages in his whole discourse, whether we consider the matter or the manner. I have not the eloquent words he employed, but the effect of them was to impress upon the mind that as Poetry might in some sort be considered the language of Heaven, so the enjoyment of it, that exquisite delight we received from it, was a sort of type or prophecy of a future happy and blissful existence.

Another cause of false criticism was the greater purity of our morals in

---

[1] *Scotch professorial Court*] Presumably Coleridge had in mind the group of Scottish critics and rhetoricians who flourished towards the end of the eighteenth century, and many of whom were professors at one of the universities in Scotland; among them were George Campbell, James Beattie, and, perhaps the best known, Hugh Blair, whose *Lectures on Rhetoric* were published in 1783. The reference is omitted from the 1856 text.

[2]] In this paragraph Coleridge seems to be recorded as quoting from the lectures he gave in 1808 at the Royal Institution. In a letter of 21 May 1808 addressed to Wordsworth (*Letters*, III, 111), he said he was about to lecture on modern poetry and on Wordsworth himself, but there is no evidence that he did so, and he may have abandoned the course at about this point because of illness. The evidence, however, is confused, for in *Biographia Literaria* (1817), I, 38, Coleridge says he confined himself in the 1808 lectures to the poetry of the past, from Chaucer to Thomson, while in a later letter of 1818 to William Mudford, and again in a note dated 7 or 17 January 1819, and written on a blank leaf in his copy of Stockdale's edition of Shakespeare (1807; B.M.C.61.h.7; printed in *Literary Remains*, II, 202–3, and in Raysor, I, 16–17 (18–19)), he says he gave eighteen lectures on Shakespeare. The plan called for twenty-five lectures, on Shakespeare and other poets, and if he gave only eighteen, then he did not lecture on modern poetry, which was due to be the subject commencing in Lecture 19 of the series.

The paragraph Collier reports here, however, suggests that Coleridge may, after all, have said something about his contemporaries. It is much changed in the 1856 text (Raysor, II, 58 (34)), and the reference to the 1808 lectures is omitted.

the present age, which, he maintained, however vilified, was in morality superior to the last. Who now would venture to read even a number from the Spectator or the Tatler to his wife or daughters without first examining it to see if there were any improper sentences, not fit for the delicacy of female ears? Even our theatres, that in general fixed the morals, had taken a domestic turn, and while the representations improved the hearts, [they] injured the taste of the Auditory. It was a bad cause, but an excellent effect.

It had been attempted to write systems of Education, but they appeared to him like Greek and Latin Grammars put into the hands of Schoolboys, which, including all the minutiae of language, taught them to judge before they had the means of judging. These were the principal accidental causes.

The *Permanent causes* were

1. The great[er] pleasure we feel in being told of the knowledge we possess than of the ignorance we labour under. Under this division he introduced a simile between a person who taught thinking and a Chamois Hunter in the Alps. The man who followed the Chamois Hunter saw him ascend the steepest precipices without injury, leap from crag to crag without alarm, and accomplish his object without apparent difficulty, but the follower found that without himself exerting the same energies, calling forth the like perseverance, and displaying alike intrepidity, his chase would be vain, and his efforts fruitless. Systems had been produced with the avowed object of instructing men how to think, but in his opinion their proper title should have been 'a system to teach men how to think without thinking'.*

He impressed with warmth upon his hearers the propriety of cultivating the thinking faculties that we might properly fill the duties of our station. On man God had not only bestowed gifts, but the *power of giving*: he was not like the creature of a mere created being, that was born but to die; he had had faculties communicated to him which were beneficial to others. Man might be considered in a secondary sense *his own creator*, for by the improvement of the faculties given him by God, he enlarged them, and even created new ones.

The second cause was the habit, which people had, of judging of books by books. This was in some sort connected with what he had observed regarding reviews. People did not exert their own abilities, but being by nature inclined to sloth rather than judge and decide for themselves, they took for granted the opinions of others. This had been the

---

* A familiar illustration might have been that it was like teaching an infant to run before it had been instructed to walk.

case with a friend of his, who observed that he did not think Shakespeare had made Constance in King John speak the language of nature where she said, on the loss of Prince Arthur,

> Grief fills the room [up] of my absent child,
> Lies in his bed, walks up and down with me,
> Puts on his pretty looks, repeats his words,
> Remembers me of all his gracious parts,
> Stuffs out his vacant garments with his form;
> Then have I reason to be fond of grief.

Within three months after he had made this remark the friend died. Coleridge went to see his mother, an ignorant though amiable woman, who had scarcely heard the name of Shakespeare, much less read him. Coleridge, like King Philip in the Play alluded to, attempted to console her, and in reply, in the bitter anguish of her grief, she uttered almost a parody on the language of Shakespeare, employing the same thoughts and little varied in the phrazeology.*

A third permanent cause was the vague use of terms. Here he took occasion to impress upon his hearers the necessity of using only appropriate expressions even in common conversation, and in the ordinary transactions of life. He exemplified this head by adducing the word *Taste*, the use of which had been so much abused and misapplied, as well as the epithets, sublime, majestic, grand, striking, picturesque, etc. He related the following anecdote[1]—he was surveying the fall of the Clyde, and was ruminating on what epithet could be best applied to it, and after much deliberation he pitched upon Majestic as the proper one. While he was still engaged on it a gentleman and lady came up, neither of whose faces bore much of the stamp of wisdom, and the first word the gentleman uttered was, 'It is very majestic'. Coleridge was much pleased to find a concurrent opinion, and complimented the person on the choice of his term in warm language. 'Yes, Sir', replies the gentleman, 'I say it is very majestic, it is sublime, and it is beautiful, and it is grand, and picturesque'—'Aye,' added the lady, 'it is the prettiest thing I ever saw.' Coleridge was not a little disconcerted.

* I recollect that Coleridge made this observation when dining with us, and I think I must have noticed it elsewhere, but at present I cannot find it. I think I have heard him *say* other things that he repeated in his lecture.

---

[1] *anecdote*] This was a favourite anecdote; a version was used in the 1808 lectures (Raysor, I, 162 (182)), and other forms of it appear in *Biographia Literaria*, II, 224–5, and in *Table-Talk*, 24 June 1827 (printed in Raysor, 1930 text only, II, 352).

He here laid by his lecture, and taking up his prospectus,[1] he adverted to what he had there advertized, that his Lectures, as well as being 'in illustration of the principles of Poetry', would comprize 'their application as grounds of criticism to the most popular works of later English Poets, those of the living included'. He remarked that in examining the merits, whether comparative or otherwise, of his contemporaries, he should dismiss all feelings that could lead him to deduce anything but a right conclusion. He should give talent and genius, where it was shown, its due praise, and only bestow censure where truth and justice required it. He read a passage from one of his works, I rather think his own lectures at the Royal Institution, relative to impartiality to living authors,[2] and concluded by declaring that in pursuing this object he should not fear an accusation of arrogance and presumption from the good and the wise; he should pity it in the weak, and despise it in the wicked.

Such was the introductory lecture, and it might not be impertinent to say that I was disappointed in two respects, both of which, I dare say, will be remedied as Coleridge proceeds; I mean, in the delivery, which was defective, and in the brilliance, which was not dazzling. It was not quite equal to what I expected from Coleridge, though superior to what could have been delivered by any other man.

Tuesday November 19th[3]

I have been told of the following remark, or rather bon mot, or what you please to call it, made or said by Coleridge. He was endeavouring to account for Scotchmen wishing to be called Scotsmen, and it was in this way: he said that it arose from a natural aversion to the sound of the letters *ch*, which reminded them of the principal characteristic (if he might so call it) of their countrymen. We know it in England by the name of the *Scotch* Fiddle,[4] but why it is so called I know not, unless it be (which I think is not improbable) that when they rub their backs against the scrubbing posts which used to be regularly set up on the road

---

[1] *prospectus*] Coleridge quotes accurately from it; see above, p. viii.

[2] *lectures . . . living authors*] See above, p. 47 and n. The two references seem to indicate that Coleridge delivered at any rate one lecture on modern poetry in May or June 1808, though no other evidence survives. Like the earlier one, this reference to the 1808 lectures was omitted from the 1856 text (Raysor, II, 63 (38)).

[3] *Tuesday November 19th*] The text from here to the heading 'Second Lecture' was not printed by Collier in 1856. It is interesting in itself, and shows how these first two lectures were written up as entries in his diary.

[4] *Scotch Fiddle*] i.e. the itch.

like milestones, it gave the elbows of the person scrubbing much the same action that a man has when he is fiddling. This reminds me of an old story of a *Scots*man who saw a pig scratching his back under a gate. He immediately flew into a passion, pulled out his family knife, and crying 'Nae Reflaetions' stuck the poor animal.

This saying of Coleridge is more like Chas Lamb, who is constantly bringing out some drollery or other; you may say of him what Goldsmith says of Whitehead,[1] 'Who relished a joke and rejoiced at a pun'. I have heard him make some that are extremely excellent.

This Evening I went to the Philological Society. The question to be debated was 'whether women possessed minds inferior to those of men ?' Of course I spoke, but on entering the room I found that the side of the question I had adopted would meet with too many supporters, so I resolved to try to turn my attention to the other. I felt convinced that the intellects of women were equal to those of men, and their moral feelings superior, but I wished to convince that men in both were superior. I set myself therefore to think, but after debating in my own mind for some time, and arranging my ideas in favour of the men, I gave it up, and resolved to pursue my natural bent in favour of the women. I thus [so] puzzled myself between what I ought to say and what I wished that I said neither what I ought or wished, and made a bad speech of what might have been a good one. I will do myself the justice, however, to say that there were good points in it. I terminated with a quibble fit for a peroration; I trusted to chance, and chance brought me out of the scrape with some éclat. In allusion to the practice of showing hands to decide the question I observed that it was impossible for any man to raise his hand against a female. Posterity, are you of my opinion ?

The debate terminated by a division contrary to my wishes. The principal contention was between Will Andrews and a Mr. Taylor, but it was quite obvious that the former was striving against the stream, and would fain have turned to flood with it. It was on the whole a dull discussion.

Wednesday November 20th

Read Milton as usual.

There are two passages[2] in which there is exactly the same thought

---

[1] *Whitehead*] The line in fact occurs in the 'Postscript' added in the second issue of the fourth edition of Goldsmith's poem 'Retaliation' (1774), as an epitaph on Caleb Whitefoord, who probably wrote the lines himself; see *Collected Works of Oliver Goldsmith*, ed. Arthur Friedman (1966), IV, 345–6. The text may be found in *The Works of Oliver Goldsmith*, ed. Peter Cunningham (1854), I, 84.

[2] *passages*] *Paradise Lost*, I, 203 ('the side' should read 'his side'), and VII, 412.

repeated. It relates to the whale. The first occurs in *Par. L.* 1. 1 and is a comparison of Satan on the flaming sea to a Leviathan slumbering on the ocean:

> Him haply slumbering on the Norway foam,
> The Pilot of some small night-foundered skiff,
> Deeming some island, oft, as seamen tell,
> With fixed anchor in his scaly rind,
> Moors by the side under the lee, etc.

The other occurs in the 7th book:

> there Leviathan
> Hugest of living creatures on the deep
> Stretched like a promontory, sleeps or swims
> And seems a moving land.

Thursday November 21st

Read Milton as usual.

This evening Coleridge delivered his second Lecture, which is not only beyond my praise, but beyond the praise of any man, but himself. He only is capable of speaking of himself. All others seem so contemptible in comparison. I felt myself more humble if possible than the meanest worm before the Almighty, and blessed my stars that I could comprehend what he had the power to invent. But let Coleridge speak for himself.

Second Lecture

He began by observing that Readers might be divided into four classes.[1]

1. Sponges: persons who absorbed what they read and returned it nearly in the same state, only a little dirtied.

2. Sand-glasses, who permitted everything to pass away and were contented to doze away their time in actual idleness.

3. Strain-bags, who retained only the dregs of what they received.

4. Great Mogul Diamonds who were equally rare and valuable.

The principal complaint against moderns was the laxity in the use of

---

[1] *four classes*] In the 1856 text (Raysor, II, 64 (39)), the description of the four classes was much altered, and the version given here appears to be a far more accurate record of what Coleridge said, for it more or less coincides with surviving manuscript notes for part of this lecture; see Raysor, I, 249–52 (220–2).

terms, to which he had adverted in his last lecture, by which language became corrupted—For instance, the word *indorsed*, which had been so misapplied, when its true signification was given by Milton,[1] where he says 'And Elephants *indorsed* with towers.' The word Virtue had been equally perverted. Originally it signified merely strength—It then became the strength of the mind or valour and it was now changed to the class term of modern[2] excellence in all its various species. At the same time that he recommended more precision, he did not mean to say that we should labour after a constant precision where it was not wanted. What men had principally to attend to was to distinguish subtly that we might be afterwards able to assimilate truly.

He had often heard the question put whether Pope was a great Poet, and warmly discussed on both sides, but the parties never thought of enquiring what was meant by the words *Poet* or *Poetry*. He illustrated this sentiment further by an allusion to *Gulliver's Travels*, which I did not exactly comprehend.[3] In morals, politics, or philosophy, it was absolutely necessary to explain the terms employed in the first instance. It was therefore requisite that he should explain what was to be understood by the term *Poetry* before he entered upon the comparative merits of any of those who were called Poets.

Words were used in 2 ways:

1. In a sense which comprizes every thing called by that name. For instance, the words Poetry and sense were employed in this sense when we say such a sentence is *bad poetry*, or bad sense, when in truth it was neither poetry or sense at all. The same remark he applied to Metre.

2. A Philosophic Sense, which must include a definition of what is essential to the thing. No one meant in reality merely metre by Poetry. Something more was wanted—It was not wit: we might have wit where we never dreamt of Poetry. Was it just observation of human life? Was it a peculiar selection of words? This would indeed come nearer to the taste of the present age, where sound was preferred to sense, which taste he was happy to say was fast waning. The Greeks and the Romans in their latter ages were entirely ignorant of it. In the Attis of Catullus[4] it

---

[1] *Milton*] Citing *Paradise Regained*, III, 329.

[2] *modern*] Changed in 1856 to 'moral', with a footnote expressing Collier's confidence that Coleridge said this word, but stating also that his 'short-hand note' reads 'modern'.

[3] *Gulliver's Travels . . . comprehend*] Apparently Collier thought he did comprehend it in 1856, where the text is changed to, 'Poetry is not merely invention: if it were, Gulliver's Travels would be poetry' (Raysor, II, 65 (40)).

[4] *Attis of Catullus*] Collier in fact wrote 'Agis', but Coleridge must have been referring to the lament of Attis in Poem LXIII. In 1856 the title of the poem

was impossible that more simple language could be used: there was scarcely a line that a lamenting mother in a cottage might not have used. He would give of Poetry the following Definition—

It is an art (or whatever better term our language may offer) of representing in words external nature and human thoughts and affections, both relatively to human affections, by the production of as much immediate pleasure as is compatible with the largest possible sum of pleasure in the whole.

Or, to vary the words in order to make the abstract idea more intelligible,—

The art of communicating whatever we wish to communicate so as both to express and to produce excitement, but for the purpose of immediate pleasure, and so far [as] each part is fitted to afford as much pleasure as is compatible with the largest sum in the whole.

His reasons for this definition were the following:

'*It is a representation of Nature*', but that is not enough: the anatomist and the topographist give equally representations of nature; therefore I add,

'*And of the human affections*',—Here the metaphysician interferes: here our best novelists interfere likewise, excepting that the latter describe with more truth, minuteness, and accuracy than is consistent with Poetry. I subjoin consequently,

'*It must be relative to the human affections*'. Here my chief point of difference is the novel-writer and Historian, and all those who describe not only nature and the human affections, but relatively to the human affections; therefore I must add,

'*And, it must be done for the purpose of immediate pleasure*'. In Poetry the general good is to be given through the Pleasure, and if the Poet does not do that he ceases so far to be a Poet to him to whom he gives it not. Still it is not enough because we might point out the works of many prose writers to whom all the definition hitherto given would apply. I add then that it is not only for the purpose of immediate pleasure, but

'The work must be so constructed as to produce in each part that highest quantity of pleasure, or a high quantity of pleasure'. Here Metre introduces its claims, where the feeling calls for it. Our language gives it a certain measure, and will, in a strong state of passion, admit of scansion from the very mouth. The very assumption that we are reading the works of a Poet supposes that he is in a continuous state of excitement, and thereby arises a language in prose unnatural, but in poetry natural.

---

was omitted, and Collier added a footnote saying 'Coleridge here named some particular poem by Catullus; but what it was is not stated' (Raysor, II, 66 (41)).

There is one thing which ought [to be] peculiarly guarded against, which Young Poets are apt to fall into, and which old Poets fall into from their being no Poets, and who are desirous of the end true Poets seek to obtain—No, I revoke the words: they are not anxious for that of which their little minds can have no conception. They have no desire of fame, that glorious immortality of true greatness, but they seek for reputation, that echo of an echo in who[se] very etymon its signification is contained.

It was into this error that the Author of the *Botanic Garden* had fallen, Coleridge added, through the whole of which there were not to be found 20 images which were described as they would be described by a man in a state of excitement.*[1]

It was written with all the industry of a Milliner or tradesman, who was anxious to dress his ideas in silks and satins by collecting all the sonorous and handsome-looking words. He subjoined therefore to his definition,

'*As much pleasure in each part as is compatible with the greatest sum of pleasure in the whole*'.

In reading the works of Milton scarcely a line would be found that in itself would be called good. Milton[2] would not have attempted to produce what is called a good line: he sought to produce glorious paragraphs and systems of harmony, or as he expressed it,

---

* Perhaps Coleridge is just on the whole in his condemnation of the Botanic Garden, but it certainly has some fine lines, for instance (I forget what part of the work they are taken from), the following: 'Roll on ye stars, exult in youthful prime, Mark with bright curves the printless steps of time'

> Near and more near your beamy cars approach,
> And lessening orbs on lessening orbs encroach.
> Flowers of the sky! ye too to age must yield,
> Frail as your silken sisters of the field.
> Star after star from Heaven's high vault shall rush,
> Suns sink on suns, and systems systems crush,
> Headlong extinct to one dark centre fall,
> And death and night and chaos mingle all,
> Till o'er the wreck emerging from the storm,
> Immortal nature lifts her changeful form,
> Mounts from her funeral pyre on wings of flame,
> And shines and soars, another and the same.

---

[1] *excitement*] Collier added here a superfluous 'would describe', which I have omitted. The footnote he also added does not appear in the 1856 text. He cites, with some minor inaccuracies, *The Botanic Garden*, Part 1, 'The Economy of Vegetation', Canto IV, 367–80. In this passage, Erasmus Darwin is celebrating Herschel's discovery of nebulae, and his theories about them. In l. 5 'vault' should read 'arch', and in the last line 'shines and soars' should read 'soars and shines'.

[2] *Milton*] Citing 'L'Allegro', 139.

With many a bout
Of linked sweetness long drawn out.*

Such as he had defined it, in future lectures he should consider the sense of the word *Poetry*. Pleasurable excitement was its origin and object; pleasure formed the magic circle out of which the Poet never dare attempt to tread. The definition he had supplied would apply equally to Painting and to Music as to Poetry, but to the [last] must be added *words and metre*, and the definition was distinctly and solely applicable to Poetry, which produced that delight which was the parent of many virtues. When he was in Italy a friend of his who pursued painting with the highest enthusiasm, believing it to [be] superior to everything, on hearing this definition confessed the superiority of Poetry.†

Coleridge here alluded to the acute sensations of pain he experienced on beholding the Cartoons of Raphael and 'the Florentine'[1] at Rome, when he reflected that their being painted in Fresco was the only reason why they yet remained, and had not, like others, become the victims of insatiate avarice or wanton barbarity. How grateful, he exclaimed, should we be that the works of Euclid and Plato still remained to us, and that we were yet possessed of those of Newton, of Milton, and of Shakespeare, the great *living dead* men of our island, and that they would not now be in danger of a second eruption of the Goths and Vandals. They will never cease to be admired till man shall cease to exist, and at the present moment the greatest name our isle can boast had but received the first fruits of his glory, which glory must for ever increase wherever our language is spoken.[2] Some prejudices have been attached to the name of our illustrious countryman which it will be necessary for me first to attempt to obviate. On the Continent the works of Shakespeare are

* On talking over this matter, Mr. Robinson observed that Shelley,[3] a musical composer, had found this fault with Haydn's Creation, where, instead of making the Oratorio one beautiful expressive whole, he had paid too much attention to the particular parts, and to make every sound descriptive of some part of the operation of creation. The same fault was found with Handel.

† Coleridge here must have alluded to a young Englishman he met with in Italy, of the name I think of Miers.[4] He noticed him at my father's Table.

---

[1] *the Florentine*] Michaelangelo, whose name is substituted in the 1856 text (Raysor, II, 69 (43)).

[2] This passage is much expanded in the 1856 text, and includes a reference to Ben Jonson's Epitaph on the Countess of Pembroke, according to Collier's note there (Raysor, II, 69–70 (43–4)).

[3] *Shelley*] Possibly an error for William Shield (1748–1829), a well-known composer, who was acquainted with Haydn. But there is no allusion to him in *Henry Crabb Robinson on Books and their Writers*.

[4] *Miers*] Unidentified. This note is not in the 1856 text.

honoured in a double way; by the admiration of Italy and Germany, and by the contempt of the French.

Coleridge here read a Passage from, I think, Theobald,[1] on the nature of Shakespeare's mind, in which it was said that he seemed a great man in his own despite, and that where he was not much above all other writers, that he was equally below them: that he was a man of an irregular mind; that he was a sort of *lusus naturae* and at other times was called a mere child of nature.*

Such was the language employed by those who thought Sophocles the great model for Tragedy, and Aristotle its great censor, and, finding that *Hamlet, King Lear, Macbeth,* and other of Shakespeare's Tragedies [were] not framed in the same mould, and not having courage to deny the justness of that model, or the propriety of those rules, have asserted that Shakespeare was a sort of irregular writer, that he was tasteful but incorrect, and that he was a mere child of nature.

It was an old, and hitherto he had esteemed it a just Latin maxim, '*Oportet discentem credere, edoctum judicare*',[2] but modern practice had so perverted the sense that [it] ought rather now to stand 'Oportet discentem judicare, edoctum credere', and for this mistake, or rather infatuation, there was but one remedy, viz; the acquirement of knowledge. He had often applied to the ignorant who assumed the province of judges a ludicrous but not inapt simile. They reminded him of frogs croaking in a ditch or bog involved in darkness, but the moment a lantern were brought near the scene of their disputing society they ceased their discordant harangues. At other times they reminded him of the night-fly which fluttered round the glimmering of every feeble taper, but were overpowered by the dazzling glory of the noon. Nor would it be otherwise until the idea were exploded that knowledge can be easily taught, and until we learnt the first great truth, that to conquer ourselves is the only true knowledge.

* Calling Shakespeare a child of nature seems to me his highest praise as applied to a Dramatic poet whose object is or ought to be to represent only nature.

---

[1] *Theobald*] It was not Theobald. Coleridge was no doubt quoting here from Pope's 'Epistle to Augustus', 1, 72, where it is said Shakespeare 'grew immortal in his own despite', and from his preface to *The Works of Shakespeare* (1725), where he wrote, 'with all these great excellencies he has almost as great defects; and that as he has certainly written better, so he has perhaps written worse, than any other'; Pope also said, 'he is not so much an Imitator, as an Instrument, of Nature' (*Eighteenth Century Essays on Shakespeare*, ed. D. Nichol Smith, 46, 44). In the 1856 text the reference to Theobald is omitted, and some of the ideas attributed to him are assigned instead to 'the French' (Raysor, II, 70 (44)).

[2] *Oportet . . . judicare*] i.e. a man should have faith while learning, and exercise judgment when he is educated.

Plato called the mathematical Sciences the[1]
Coleridge in the strongest manner censured the practice of teaching mathematics by making the illustrations obvious to the senses. We should think and not feel.

It was owing to this deficiency that Shakespeare had been too difficult for the comprehension of such persons.

It was his purpose to show in the next place the state of the stage, and of the times in which Shakespeare lived, in order to decide the first great question, viz; as to his judgment. If it were possible to say what one of this great man's extraordinary powers were more commendable and admirable than his other powers, it appeared to him that his judgment was the most wonderful. This opinion was formed by Coleridge after a careful comparison of Shakespeare's works with the best and greatest of his contemporaries.

If the *Lear* were to be tried by those rules on which Sophocles constructed his *Oedipus*, it must be admitted that it was a very irregular piece. If it were allowed that Aristotle's rules were founded on man and nature, undoubtedly Shakespeare must be condemned for arraying his works in charms with which, according to those rules, they ought never to have been decorated. Coleridge however had no fear that he should be able to show that the great men of Greece and the great man of England proceeded in the same process.

The lecturer here entered into an account of the Origin of ancient dramatic representations, particularly Tragedy, from the celebration of the feasts of Bacchus, which is also given in a very clear and excellent manner in Goldsmith's *Essay on the Origin of Poetry*.[2] The same author gives the rise and progress of Comedy.

The Unities, he added, originated in the size and origin of the ancient theatres, and were made to include within a short space of time events which it was impossible could have occurred in that short space of time, and they could not be fit and true, unless it were possible to imagine all theatrical representations ideal. If mere pain for the moment were wanted, could we not go to our hospitals; if we required mere pleasure, could we not be present at our public fêtes? This was not what was

---

[1] *the*] Collier left the sentence unfinished. No reference to Plato appears in the 1856 text here.

[2] *Essay on the Origin of Poetry*] This essay, which first appeared in *The British Magazine* in 1762, and was included in *Essays and Criticisms, by Dr. Goldsmith* (1798), is no longer attributed to Goldsmith; it may be found in *The Works of Oliver Goldsmith*, ed. Cunningham (1854), III, 302–7. This entire paragraph, including the reference to Goldsmith, is omitted from the 1856 text (Raysor, II, 72 (46)).

required from dramatic exhibition: we wanted a continual representation of it before our eyes. The real pleasure derived was from knowing that the scene represented was unreal and merely an imitation.

He went on to notice the unnatural and unmusical stretch of voice required in large theatres, and the introduction of Recitative for the purpose of making pleasantly artificial the distortion of the voice occasioned by the magnitude of the building.

The origin of the English Theatre, he remarked, was less boastful than that of the Greeks, like the Constitution by which we were governed, which, though more barbarous in its derivation, gave more genuine and diffused liberty than Athens in the height of her political glory ever possessed.—He here noticed the Ancient Religious mysteries, filled with blasphemies that the most hardened to vice in the present day dared not utter. In these performances Vice and the Devil were personified, and from thence arose the introduction of our Fool and Clown.

Shakespeare, at the same time that he accommodated himself to the taste of the times, employed these characters to a most terrible effect in heightening the misery of his most distressing scenes. He quoted a passage from a Paper written by a friend, which observed upon the high colouring given by contrast to the Scene where Lear, in the very pitch of his agony, complaining to the elements and accusing them of ingratitude, is mocked by the mimicry of the fool, his only attendant in his calamities.[1] (Note) It may not be amiss here to say something on what Dr Johnson has so well observed regarding the unities of Time, Place, and Action, whose steps on this subject Coleridge is but following. . . .[2]

Friday November 22nd[3]

I was employed during my leizure hours this day in writing out Coleridge's Lecture[4] principally; at intervals read Milton.

---

[1] *calamities*] This passage is rather changed in the 1856 text, which has an additional short paragraph on Shakespeare's 'loftier' purpose than his contemporaries in using clowns (Raysor, II, 74 (47)).

[2] *following*] Collier went on to copy out a well-known passage from the preface to Dr. Johnson's edition of Shakespeare (1765), in which he dismisses the unities, and says 'spectators are always in their senses, and know, from the first act to the last, that the stage is only a stage, and the players are only players.' This does not appear in the 1856 text, and there seemed no point in reprinting it here.

[3] *November 22nd*] This and the following entries up to that of Wednesday, 27 November 1811, bring Collier's diary to an end. The remaining pages of this fourth brochure are blank, and Brochure 5 opens with a transcription of Lecture 6. These diary entries were not printed by Collier in 1856, or by Raysor.

[4] *lecture*] i.e. Lecture 2, delivered on Thursday 21 November.

Saturday November 23rd

I forget—Read Milton.

Sunday November 24th

Heard a good, but diffuse and desultory, sermon from Belsham[1] on the duty imposed upon those who were learned to instruct those who were ignorant—After the sermon he renewed his Lectures. I will endeavour to give an account of it at a future time.

Monday November 25th

Heard Coleridge's third Lecture,[2] and employed myself in transcribing my Notes: q: v:—

Tuesday November 26th

Transcribing Coleridge's Lecture occupied me all day—

Miss Andrews and the Bakewells all came in the Evening—Dull. I am quite out of my element with young people.

Wednesday November 27th

Bought Barron's Essays.[3]

In the Evening went to C. Lamb's—present—

G. Dyer[4]—W. Hazlitt—C. Lamb—Phillips[5]—Rickman*[6] M. Burney[7]—Capt. Burney,[8] Miss Lamb.[9]

* not performed Clio.

---

[1] *Belsham*] Thomas Belsham (1750–1829), noted Unitarian minister and author of numerous published sermons and discourses.

[2] *third lecture*] Collier's notes and transcription are lost. In a note at the end of Lecture 2 as printed in 1856 Collier expressed his regret that he had not recovered his notes for Lectures 3, 4 and 5 (Raysor, II, 77 (47)).

[3] *Barron's Essays*] Presumably William Barron's *Lectures on Belles Lettres and Logic*, 2 vols., 1806.

[4] *G. Dyer*] George Dyer (1755–1841), poet and friend of Lamb.

[5] *Phillips*] Probably Edward Phillips, a friend of Lamb.

[6] *Rickman*] John Rickman (1771–1840), parliamentary official and friend of Southey, not (as Collier's note makes clear), the bookseller and adherent of Tom Paine, Thomas Rickman (1761–1834), who wrote under the name of 'Clio'.

[7] *M. Burney*] Martin Burney, son of Captain James Burney, and nephew of Fanny Burney (Madame D'Arblay).

[8] *Capt. Burney*] James, later Admiral Burney, brother of Fanny Burney, and son of Dr Charles Burney, the historian of music.

[9] *Miss Lamb*] Mary, Charles Lamb's sister.

G. Dyer. The ancients called Wisdom σοφία Pythagoras was the first who called it φιλοσοφία—He did not know what was meant when persons used the Phraze 'Philosophy of the mind'.

W. Hazlitt. Censured Coleridge much for not at least making his definition of Poetry distinct and clear.

Rickman did not wonder at it because he (Coleridge) did not understand it himself. He had better never have attempted to define it at all. Definitions were always difficult to make, difficult to be understood, and frequently not necessary or worth understanding.

W. Hazlitt thought that Coleridge had failed in his attempt—To his mind Poetry appeared something between words and music, and the question was, what justified a man in combining the two. Coleridge said a state of excitement. He (Hazlitt) did not know, but it seemed to him that a Poet was like a man on horseback on a rough road, who, instead of travelling on among the ruts and ruggedness, preferred the greensward at the side.

C. Lamb remarked that with regard to one point, that respected the Unities, Coleridge was original, viz. in what he said regarding the Chorus being always on the stage, which prevented the change of the Scene. He praised the manner in which Coleridge had shown that the Unities were owing to accidents.

W. Hazlitt wished to remind Coleridge of Dr Sam Johnson[1] of Litchfield who, if he recollected rightly, had said something on the same subject.

It was remarked that Dr Johnson founded his overthrow of the ancient unities of Time and Place on the point that the audience did not imagine that the proceedings on the stage were reality. In one place he had said that if the audience fancied any persons in a tragedy unhappy, it was themselves and not the actors.

W. Hazlitt did not think Coleridge at all competent to the task he had undertaken of lecturing on Shakespeare, as he was not well read in him. He knew little more than was in the Elegant Extracts, and Hazlitt himself had told him of many beautiful passages that Coleridge had never before heard of. It was owing to this ignorance that Coleridge had not exemplified any of his positions by quoting passages, and he doubted if he ever would—Milton he was well acquainted with, and some years ago his readings of him were very fine; his natural whine gave them effect: this whine had since grown upon him and was now disagreeable.

---

[1] *Johnson*] In the Preface to his edition of Shakespeare; see *The Works of Samuel Johnson*, ed. A. Sherbo, VII, 76–80.

Coleridge was a man who had more ideas than any other person Hazlitt had ever known, but had no capability of attending to one object; he was constantly endeavouring to push matters to the furthest till he became obscure to everybody but himself. He was like a man who, instead of cultivating and bringing to perfection a small plot of ground, was attempting to cultivate a whole tract, but instead of accomplishing his object dug up the ground only for the encouragement of weeds.

G. Dyer thought that Coleridge was the fittest man for a Lecturer he had ever known: he was constantly lecturing when in company, only he did it better.

C. Lamb objected to what Coleridge had said on Shakespeare, when he remarked that it was the Poet we saw in every character, that though we beheld the Nurse or the blundering Constable, it was not those characters only, but the Poet transferring himself to those characters. If he had said that it was the Poet who spoke in the characters of Shallow or Slender or Sir Hugh Evans it would have been much better, as there was nothing very original in the characters Coleridge alluded to: there was in those he omitted.

W. Hazlitt put the characters of Coleridge and Roscoe in contrast. The one was a man full of ideas but of no industry, the other a man of great industry and no ideas. This was the merit of Roscoe's[1] life of Lorenzo de' Medici, that he had collected with great labour all the materials, and had employed them with much exertion to advantage. Coleridge's mind was full of materials for building, but he had not perseverance to employ those he had, but, always fancying himself deficient, was in the constant search for more.

During the Evening the conversation turned upon Johnson. *Mr. Burney* praised his *Vanity of Human Wishes* above his *London*.

W. Hazlitt thought Wordsworth's Criticism[2] upon the two first lines,

Let observation with extensive view
Survey mankind from China to Peru,

extremely just, viz. that the first was wholly unnecessary, as the complete idea to be expressed was contained in the second line.

Phillips was a great admirer of Johnson. Boswell's life of Johnson

---

[1] *Roscoe's*] William Roscoe, whose *Life of Lorenzo de' Medici* appeared in 1795, and was in its fifth edition by 1806.

[2] *Wordsworth's Criticism*] Made perhaps in conversation. Wordsworth criticizes a poem by Dr Johnson in the Preface to *Lyrical Ballads*, but does not cite this passage. Coleridge, however, makes the same point about *The Vanity of Human Wishes* in Lecture 6 (see below, p. 70).

would have been nearly as great a loss as Johnson's works, because all the Doctor's good sayings would have been lost. Boswell said nothing good himself.

W. Hazlitt said that Boswell was a Scotsman, and a Blackguard of course.

Capt. Burney asked if it necessarily followed that because a man was a Scotsman that he was a blackguard.

W. Hazlitt as naturally as that an African should be a black.

M. Burney praised Juvenal and quoted some lines.

C. Lamb had compared Halliday's[1] translation of Persius and found it better than the original.

---

[1] *Halliday's*] Untraced. Possibly the anonymous translation of Persius published in 1806.

4

The transcript of Lecture 6

Coleridge's Sixth Lecture

He commenced by making some further remarks upon education, and the practice of inflicting corporal punishment on children, which in his opinion had no tendency to degrade or debase the infant's mind, in as much as they saw that all, even the Judges of the land, and the greatest and most revered characters, had been subjected to it. He noticed an advertizement that he had seen about 20 years ago published by a Schoolmaster[1] in which he assured the tender parents that [he would use no] corporal chastisement excepting in cases of absolute necessity, and that even then it should be inflicted only with lilies and roses stripped of their thorns. What was the consequence of the abolition of flogging? In endeavouring to remove a pimple, the disease had been transferred to the very vitals, for the moral feelings had been attacked. A man of great reputation (he should rather say notoriety) had punished those under his care sometimes by suspending them from the ceiling in baskets to be the derision of his Schoolfellows: at other times he had fastened round the boy a number of last dying speeches and confessions, and employed another of his pupils to go before him making the usual lamentation heard in the streets. This punishment was imposed because a boy read with a tone,[2] which led him to observe that reading in a tone was strictly natural and truly proper, excepting in the excess. What would a parent think if he saw his child punished in the way he had described: where

[1] *Schoolmaster*] Joseph Lancaster (1778–1838), the noted educational reformer (so Raysor).

[2] *tone*] i.e. intonation, a special or affected manner. Collier noted in 1856 that this was Coleridge's own way of reading verse (Raysor, II, 112 (81)).

the feelings of the child were connected and associated with the sentence of the most abandoned criminal? After dwelling for some time on propriety in reading, and observing that the true point of excellence is to give to everything that which belongs to it, he remarked, in allusion to delivery, that in addressing a mixed audience who are desirous of instruction, it was not as a man carrying furniture into an empty house, but as a man entering a well furnished dwelling and exhibiting a light— which enabled a man to see what was in his own mind.

Coleridge then paid a high compliment to Davy[1] (at whose desk he had had the honour of lecturing—at the Royal Institution), who had reduced the art of Chemistry to a science, [and] who had discovered one common law applicable to the mind and body, which enabled us to give a full and perfect Amen to the great axiom of Lord Bacon that knowledge is power.[2] He then observed that when he delivered his Lectures at the Royal Institution, he had prepared his first Lecture and received for it a cold suffrage of approbation: from accidental causes he was unable to study his second lecture, and obtained universal and heartfelt applause. With the same spirit he hoped the lectures he was about to deliver would be received. It was true his thoughts would not be so accurately arranged, but his audience should have the whole Skeleton, though the bones were not put together with the nicest anatomical skill.

The lecturer then dwelt for some time upon the immense advantage men of genius possessed over men of talents and men of arms, and drew a comparison between the benefits derived from the Iliad of Homer or the history of the Conquests of Alexander. Thucydides, it was true, had written the history of the Peloponnesian War, but what cared we for the Peloponnesian War? But woe be to the Statesman, he exclaimed, who had not availed himself of the wisdom contained in the tale of Troy divine.

Lord Bacon[3] had beautifully expressed this idea where he talked of the destruction and instability of the monuments of the greatest heroes,

[1] *Davy*] Altered to 'Sir Humphry Davy' in 1856. Davy was in fact knighted in April 1812, some months after this lecture was given. Andrew Brae, in his *Collier, Coleridge and Shakespeare*, noted that Collier must have altered the text at this point; see above, p. 10.

[2] *Knowledge is power*] The phrase is taken from Bacon's 'Of Heresies' in his *Religious Meditations* (*Works*, ed. Spedding, Ellis and Heath, 1861, VII, 253).

[3] *Bacon*] In *The Advancement of Learning*, Bk. I, viii, 6: 'We see then how far the monuments of wit and learning are more durable than the monuments of power or of the hands. For have not the verses of Homer continued twenty-five hundred years, or more, without the loss of a syllable, or letter . . . how much more are letters to be magnified, which as ships, pass through the vast seas of time, and make ages so distant to participate of the wisdom, illuminations, and inventions, the one of the other.'

and compares them with the everlasting writings of Homer, a word of which had never been lost; which, like a mighty ship, had passed over the sea of time, though not like a ship leaving an ideal tract and had disappeared, but like a ship that had left a train of glory in its wake and was still present to us, acting upon us, ennobling us by its thoughts and images, and to it perhaps the bravest of our soldiery might attribute their heroic deeds. He felt too that, just as the body is to the immortal mind, so are the mere actions of our bodily powers in proportion to those by which, independent of individual continuity,[1] we are to be governed by for ever and ever; and not only to call the narrow circle of mankind (narrow comparatively) our brethren, but to call all who succeed us equally our brethren, and to look forward to that exalted state when we shall welcome into Heaven thousands and thousands who shall say, 'To thee I owe the first development of my imagination, to thee I owe the withdrawing of my mind from the low and brutal part of my nature to the lofty and perpetual'.

Coleridge had looked at the reign of Elizabeth, interesting on many accounts, with more especial pleasure as it furnished circumstances so favourable to the existence and full development of Shakespeare. The reformation had produced a great activity of mind, and a passion for thinking, and for making words to express the objects of thought and invention. It was consequently the age of many conceits, and an age when for a time the intellect stood above the moral sense.

It was almost miraculous to compare the state of mind in the reigns of Elizabeth and James with the reigns of Charles the 1st and 2nd, when republicanism was so prevalent. In the former period there was an amazing development of power, but all connected with prudential purposes: an attempt to reconcile the moral feeling with a full exercise of the mind and the gaining of certain ends. In that age lived Bacon and Burleigh, and Sir Walter Raleigh, and a galaxy of great men of which they formed a part. Coleridge lamented that they should have degraded their mighty powers to such base ends, and dissolve[d] their pearls in such a worthless acid, to be drunken[2] as it were to an harlot. What was the favour of a Queen or a Court to such a man as Lord Bacon but mere harlotry?

Compare this age to that of the republicans: it was an awful age

---

[1] *continuity*] In 1856 Collier altered this passage slightly, and added a footnote in which he said, 'it strikes me that something explanatory must have been accidently omitted, and perhaps that the word I have written "continuity" ought to be *contiguity*' (Raysor, II, 114–15 (83)).

[2] *drunken*] 'Drunked' in MS.

indeed, and most important as compared with our own: when England overflowed from the fullness of grand principle, from the greatness which men felt in themselves, abstracted from the prudence with which they ought to have considered whether they were adapted to mankind at large. Compare this Revolution with that of a later age, where the bubbling up and overflowing had been produced by dregs, where there was a total want of all principle, and which had raised from the bottom those dregs to the top, and founded a monarchy to be the poison and bane of the rest of mankind.

It was absolutely necessary to recollect that the age in which Shakespeare lived was one of great powers applied to prudential purposes, and not an age of high moral feeling which gains a man of genius the power of thinking of all things in reference to all. If then we should find that Shakespeare took those materials as they were, and yet to all effectual purposes produced the same grand effect as others had attempted to do in an age so much more favourable, we should then feel the holiness of genius, and that though it shone on a dunghill, still the light was as pure as the divine effluence that produced all the beauties of nature.

One of the results of the idea prevailing in that age, that persons should be men of talents in proportion as they were gentlemen, rendered certain characters of Shakespeare's drama natural with reference to the time: when we read them we know they are not of our age; they might in truth be said to be of no age. A friend of his had well remarked of Spenser that he was out of space: the reader did not know where he was, but still he knew from the consciousness within him that it was natural. So it was with Shakespeare; he was as much out of time as Spenser out of space, yet we felt that though we never knew that such characters existed, we felt conscious that they might exist.

This circumstance enabled Shakespeare to paint truly a vast multiplicity of characters by simple meditation; he had only to imitate such parts of his character, or to exaggerate such as existed in possibility, and they were at once nature, and fragments of Shakespeare. It was like men who, seeing the vast luminary of the world through various optics, some declared it to be square, triangular, or round, when in truth it was still the sun. So with the characters of our Poet, whatever forms they assumed, they were still Shakespeare, or the creatures of his meditation. When he used the term meditation, he did not mean to say that Shakespeare was without observation. Mere observation might be able to produce an accurate copy of a thing, and even furnish to other men's minds more ideas than even the copyist possessed, but they would only be in parts and in fragments: Meditation looked at every character with interest—only as it contains in it something generally true and such as might be expressed in a philosophical Problem.

Shakespeare's characters might be reduced to a few, that is to say to a few classes of characters. If you took his gentlemen for instance; the character of Biron was seen again in Mercutio, in Benedick, and a variety of others. They were men who combined the politeness of the Courtier with the faculties of intellect; the powers of combination which only belong to an intellectual mind. The wonder was how he should thus disguise himself, and have such miraculous powers of conveying the Poet, without even raising in us the consciousness of him.

In the address of Mercutio to Romeo regarding the Fairy Queen Mab (which was so well known that it was unnecessary to repeat it) there would be noticed all the fancy of the Poet, but the language in which it was contained possessing such a facility that one would say, almost, that it was impossible for it to be thought, unless it were thought as naturally and without effect as Mercutio represented it. This was the great art by which Shakespeare combined the Poet and the gentleman, throughout borrowing from his own most amiable character that which only could combine them, a perfect simplicity of mind, a delight in what was excellent for its own sake, without reference to himself as causing it, and by that which distinguished Shakespeare from all others, which is alluded to by Drummond[1] in a short poem in which he tells us that while he had the powers of a man, and more than man, yet he had all the feelings and manners which he painted in an affectionate young woman of 18.

Before he entered upon the merits of the Tragedy of Romeo and Juliet it would be necessary for him to say something of the language of the Country. Here Coleridge begged to observe however that, although he had styled these 'Lectures on Milton and Shakespeare', they were in reality intended in illustration of the principles of Poetry: therefore all must not be regarded as mere digression which did not immediately and exclusively refer to those writers, since he had chosen them in order to bring forward general truths, and whatever might [aid] himself as well as others in judging of all writers of all countries.

The language of the country could not but be regarded. It would be admitted that one language might possess advantages which another had not. It might be said that the English perhaps excelled all others in the number of its practical words. The French might bear the palm in the names of trades, and in military and diplomatic terms. Of the German

---

[1] *Drummond*] Altered in 1856 to 'one of his admirers'. No poem by William Drummond fits this description.

he would say that, exclusive of many mineralogical words, it was incomparable in its metaphysical and psychological force. In another respect it nearly rivalled the Greek, viz. in its capability of composition. Italian was the sweetest language, Spanish the most majestic. All had their peculiar faults, but he never could agree that any language was unfit for Poetry, although various languages, arising from various circumstances of the people, might fit them more for one species of Poetry than another. Take the French as an example. It was perhaps the most perspicuous and pointed language, and therefore best fitted for conversation, for the expression of light passion, attaining its object by peculiar turns of phrase which, like the beautifully coloured dust on the wings of a butterfly, must not be judged of by the touch. It appeared to have no substratum; constantly tampering with the morals, without offending the decency. As the language for what was called modern genteel comedy, all other nations must yield to them.

The Italian could only be deemed second to the Spanish, and the Spanish to the Greek, which contained the excellences of all languages. In Italian things might be represented naturally yet with dignity. As a confirmation, he appealed to Ariosto.

But in the English he saw that which was possessed by no other modern language, and which appropriated it to the Drama. It was a language composed from many, and had consequently in it many words which originally had the same meaning, but in the progress of society they had gradually assumed different shades of meaning. Take any homogeneous language, such as the Greek or the German, and try to translate the following lines of Gray:[1]

> But not to thee in this benighted age
> Is that diviner inspiration given
> Which burns in Milton's or in Shakespeare's page
> The pomp and *prodigality* of Heaven.

In German it would be necessary to say 'the pomp and spendthriftness of Heaven', because they had not, as we had, two words with nearly the same meaning, the one expressing the nobler, and the other the baser idea of the same action.

The monosyllabic character of the English Language enabled us besides to express more meaning in a shorter space than could be done in any other. In truth, it was the harvest of the unconscious wisdom of the whole nation, and was not the formation of particular individuals. Hence arose the number of passionate phrazes: the metaphorical terms

---

[1] *Gray*] Inaccurately citing *Stanzas to Bentley*, Stanza 5.

of the English language, not borrowed from the Poets, but adopted by them. He maintained that the common people, when excited by passion, constantly employed them: if a mother had lost her child she was full of the wildest fancies, the words themselves assuming a tone of dignity, for the constant hearing of the Bible and Liturgy clothed them not only in the most natural, but most beautiful forms of language.

He had been induced to make these remarks in order to obviate the objection made against Shakespeare on the ground of the multitude of his conceits. He did not pretend to justify every conceit that he had, as a vast number of the scenes attributed to Shakespeare were never written by him: but he admitted that even in those that bore the strongest characteristics of his mind there were some not strictly to be justified, but what Coleridge warned against was the notion that whenever a conceit is met with it is unnatural. Such persons forgot that they should have deemed them natural had they lived in that age. Dryden in his translation of Juvenal had said 'Look round the world'[1]—Doctor Johnson swells this out into the following lines:[2]

> Let observation with extensive view
> Survey Mankind from China to Peru.

Mere bombast and tautology, as if to say, 'Let observation with extensive observation observe mankind extensively'.

If people could throw themselves several centuries back in idea, they would find not only that conceits, but even puns were very natural. The latter generally arose from a mixture of a sense of injury and contempt, and it was a very natural way, in Coleridge's opinion, of expressing that mingled feeling. He could point out Puns in Shakespeare where they seemed, as it were, the first openings of the mouth of Nature: where nothing else could properly be said: they were like most other sentences in his works; for when you read Shakespeare, you not only feel that what he puts into the mouths of his characters might have been said, but must have been said.

In another Lecture he would state the history of conceits, and the wise use that had been made of them, and besides (which he hoped would be received with favour), he would attempt a defence of conceits and puns. He admitted that they might be misapplied, but throughout life he never had discovered the wrong use of a thing without previously

---

[1] *'Look round the world'*] Dryden's version of Juvenal's tenth satire begins, 'Look round the Habitable World'.

[2] *lines*] The opening lines of *The Vanity of Human Wishes*, also based on Juvenal's tenth satire; see also above, p. 62.

having found out the right. To the young he would say, that it was always wrong to judge of anything by its defects: the first attempt should be to discover its excellences. When a man came in to Coleridge's company and immediately began to abuse a book, while his invectives came down like water from a Shower-bath, he told him no news, because all works of course must have defects, but if he shewed him beauties he told him news indeed, because Coleridge had read many books that had nothing at all that was good. Always begin with the good. *Ab Jove principium.*

He would now speak of Shakespeare's wit, because an excellent writer,[1] who had been of great service to the public taste in driving out the nonsense of the Italian School, had said that he was surprised that all Shakespeare's other excellences were possessed by his contemporaries in a greater or less degree: Massinger had such and such a thing, Beaumont and Fletcher had more sublimity and figures, with equal knowledge of human nature, and after all he found that Shakespeare's pre-eminent quality, in which none had approached him, was his wit.[2] Coleridge felt shocked to hear it said that the something by which Shakespeare was to be individualized from all others was wit. He had read his Plays, but he confessed that the peculiar wit above all other circumstances did not strike him: he did not feel the same kind of pleasure that he had experienced on reading Voltaire, the School for Scandal, or any other witty performance.

Shakespeare had wit, it was true, but it was not to be compared to that of other writers. Shakespeare's wit blended with the other parts of his work, and was by its nature capable of being blended with them: it appeared in all parts of his works, whether tragic or comic: it was not like that of Voltaire and many modern writers, to whom the term *witty* had been properly applied, which consisted in the mere combination of words, but in Shakespeare at least 9 times out of 10 it was produced by a combination of images.

The Lecturer here drew a distinction between *Wit* and *Fancy*. When the whole pleasure received was derived from surprise at an unexpected turn of expression, then he called it *Wit*: But when the pleasure was produced not only by surprise, but likewise by an image which remained

---

[1] *writer*] William Gifford, whose *Baviad* and *Maeviad* exposed the 'Della Cruscan' poets to ridicule. Coleridge refers to Gifford's edition of Massinger in 1805, Introduction, li (Raysor's note).

[2] *Massinger . . . wit*] Altered in 1856 to include a reference to Ben Jonson; Raysor cites Gifford's words, from his introduction to *The Plays of Massinger*, li, 'Beaumont is as sublime, Fletcher as pathetick, and Jonson as nervous'.

with us, and gratified us for its own sake, then he called it *Fancy*. He knew of no other mode by which we could distinguish the signification of the words. He appealed to the recollection of his auditors whether the greater part of what passed for wit in Shakespeare was not most exquisite humour, heightened by a figure, and made humourous by being attributed to a particular character. Thus, for instance, when Falstaff saw a flea on Bardolf's nose, and compared it to a damned soul suffering in Purgatory. The images themselves in such cases afforded a great portion of the pleasure. These remarks were not without importance in forming a judgment of Poets and writers in general. There was a great distinction between that sort of talent which gave a kind of electric surprise by a mere turn of phrase, and that which produced surprise by a permanent medium, and always leaves something behind it which gratifies the mind. The first belonged to men of cleverness and talent, who, having been long in the world, had observed the turns of phrase which please in company and pass away with the moment. Of one of these men, who possessed a vast fund of this sort of talent, he had said that he was like a man who squandered away his estate in farthings, but distributed so many that he needs must have been very rich. It by no means constituted genius, though it had an affinity to it.

The Wit of Shakespeare was like the flourishing of a man's stick when he is walking along in the full flow of animal spirits. It was a sort of overflow of hilarity, which disburdened us, and seemed like a conductor to distribute a portion of our joy to the surrounding air by carrying it away from us. While too it disburdened us, it enabled us to appropriate what remained to what was most important and most within our direct aim.

He would now proceed to a most serious charge against our Poet, which was that of indecency and immorality. Many had been those who had attempted to exculpate him by saying that it was the vice of the age, but Shakespeare was too great a man to be exculpated by the accidents of any age. They had appealed to Beaumont and Fletcher, to Massinger, and to a variety of other less eminent writers in proof that it was common to all—'Oh shame and sorrow to us,' (exclaimed Coleridge), 'if it were so—there is nothing common to Shakespeare and to other writers.'

It was absolutely necessary, in order to form a proper judgment, that a distinction should be made between *manners* and *morals*, and that distinction being once clearly and distinctly comprehended, Shakespeare would appear as pure and admirable a writer, in reference to all that we ought to be, and to all that we ought to feel, as he is wonderful in reference to intellectual faculties.

By manners he meant that which was dependent on the particular customs and fashions of the age. Even in a state of comparative barbarism of manners there might be and was morality. But we had seen much worse times than those, when the mind had been so enervated and degraded, that the most distant associations that could possibly connect our ideas with the basest feelings immediately brought forward those base feelings, without referring to the nobler, thus destroying the little remnant of humanity, excluding from the mind what is good, and calling forward what is bad to keep the bestial nature company.

On looking through Shakespeare, offences against our decency and our manners might certainly be found, but examine history and observe if it was not the ordinary language existing at the time, and there could be no offence. What is most observable is that in Shakespeare it was always calculated to raise a gust of laughter that would, as it were, blow away all impure ideas or to excite disgust against them.

But above all, compare him with some of the modern writers, servile imitators of France, and it would be a most instructive lesson to us. He had made the following note after seeing a modern play he had seen represented in Malta about 9 years ago.[1]

'I went to the Theatre and returned without waiting for the entertainment. The longer I live, the more I am impressed with the exceeding immorality of modern plays. I can scarcely refrain from anger and laughter at the shamelessness or the absurdity of the presumption which presents itself when I think of their pretences to superior morality compared with the Plays of Shakespeare.'

While he was reading this note, he remembered a novel on the sopha or toilet of every woman of quality, of all immoral books the most disgusting, in which the author gravely warns parents against an indiscreet communication to their children of the contents of the Bible, as tending to injure their morality. Coleridge here burst forth into an impassioned exclamation against Monk Lewis,[2] in which he ridiculed those whose delicate sensibility could not permit the exposure of the bare leg of a Corinthian Female. My admiration almost deprived me of the power of paying attention. He then continued his note.

---

[1] *9 years ago*] Actually six or seven years previously; Coleridge was in Malta from May 1804 to September 1805 (so Raysor).

[2] *Monk Lewis*] The reference was cut in the 1856 text, which alters this sentence to: 'Another modern author, who has done his utmost to undermine the innocence of the young of both sexes, has the affrontery to protest against the exhibition of the bare leg of a Corinthian female.' M. G. Lewis's *The Monk* (1796) was attacked by Coleridge in a letter of 27 December 1802 (*Collected Letters*, II, 905), where he commented, 'My head turns giddy, my heart sickens, at the very thought of seeing such books in the hands of a child of mine'.

'In Shakespeare there are a few gross speeches, but it is doubtful to me if they would produce any ill effect on the unsullied mind, or at the worst it would be an offence only against economy; but in some of the modern *moral* plays, as well as in some novels, there is a systematic undermining of all morality; [they are] written in the true cant of humanity that has no object, where virtue is not placed in action, or in the habits that lead to action, but, like the title of a book I have heard of, they are a "hot-huddle of indefinite sensations". In those the lowest excitements to Piety are obtruded upon us: like an impudent rascal at a masquerade, who is well known in spite of his mask, or known by it yet is impudent, and is allowed to be impudent in virtue of his wearing a mask. In short, I appeal to the whole of Shakespeare's writings whether his gross is not either the mere sport of fancy, dissipating the low feeling by exciting in us intellectual feelings, and only injuring where it offends: while the modern Dramas injure in consequence of not offending. Shakespeare's worst passages are grossness against the degradations of our nature: our modern plays are too often delicacies in favour of them.'

He took the Tragedy of Romeo and Juliet because in it were to be found all the crude materials of future excellence: there was seen the Poet, the dramatic and Tragic Poet, but the various parts were not blended with such harmony as in his after writings; but still more for this reason, because it gave him the best opportunity of introducing Shakespeare as a delineator of the female character and of love in all its forms and all its emotions, which deserved the sweet and man-elevating name.

It had been remarked, Coleridge believed, by Dryden,[1] that Shakespeare wrote for men only, but Beaumont and Fletcher, or rather the gentle Fletcher, for women. He wished to begin by shewing not only that this is not true, not only that he was not inferior to Beaumont and Fletcher, but of all our writers he alone had truly drawn the female character with that mixture of the real and the ideal which belongs to woman, and that there is no one character in any of his contemporaries describing a woman, of whom a man, seriously and truly examining his heart and good sense combined in one moment, could say, 'Let that woman be my supporter in life; let her be the aid of pursuit and the reward of my success'.

---

[1] *Dryden*] Coleridge seems to be recalling Dryden's preface to *Troilus and Cressida* (*Essays of John Dryden*, ed. W. P. Ker, 1900, I, 227–8), where he remarks, 'the excellency of that poet [i.e. Shakespeare] was, as I have said, in the more manly passions; Fletcher's in the softer: Shakespeare writ better betwixt man and man; Fletcher betwixt man and woman.'

5

The transcript of Lecture 7

Coleridge's Seventh Lecture

He observed that in the former Lecture he had endeavoured to point out the union of the Poet and the Philosopher, or rather the warm embrace between them in the Venus and Adonis, and Lucrece of Shakespeare. From thence he passed on to the Love's Labour['s] Lost as the *link* between his character as a Poet and a Dramatist, and though the former was still predominant, yet the germs of Shakespeare's future dramatic excellence were discoverable.

Coleridge now proceeded to Romeo and Juliet, not because it was the earliest or among the earliest of Shakespeare's works, but because in it were to be found all his excellencies, such as they afterward appeared in his more perfect Dramas, but differing from them in being less happily combined: all the parts were present, but they were not united with the same harmony: there were many passages where the whole of his excellence was discovered, and nothing superior could be found in the productions of his after years. The distinction between this play and others was that the parts were less happily combined, or to borrow a phrase from the Painter, the whole work was less in keeping: there was the production of grand portions: there were the limbs of what was excellent; but the production of a whole, in which each part gave delight for itself, and where the whole gave more intellectual delight, was the effect of judgment and taste, not to be obtained but by painful study, and in which we gave up the stronger pleasures, derived from the dazzling light which a man of genius throws over every circumstance, and where we were chiefly struck by vivid and strong images: taste was a subsequent attainment, after the Poet had been disciplined by

75

experience, and adds to genius that talent by which he knows what part of his genius he can make intelligible to that part of mankind for whom he writes.

It would be a hopeless symptom, in Coleridge's mind, if he found a young man with a perfect taste. In the early works of Shakespeare a profusion of double epithets would be found, and sometimes the coarsest words were used if they conveyed a more vivid image, but by degrees the associations are connected with the image they are to impress, and the Poet descends from the ideal into the real world so far as to conjoin both, to give a sphere of active operations to the ideal, to elevate and refine the real.

In Romeo and Juliet the principal characters might be divided into those[1] in which passion is drawn, and drawn truly, but not individualized further than as the actor appears on the Stage: It was a very just description and development of the passion without giving, if he might so express himself, the philosophical history of it; without knowing how such a man became acted upon by that particular passion, but leading it through all the incidents and making it predominant.

Such was the character of Tybalt, which as itself was a common character: And here there was a great distinction between Shakespeare and all those who wrote in imitation of him, that Coleridge knew no character in Shakespeare, unless indeed his Pistol, which could be called mere Portraits of Individuals: while the reader felt all the delight arising from the individual, there was a sort of class character which made Shakespeare the Poet of all ages.

Of this kind was the character of Tybalt, a man abandoned to his passions, and with all the pride of family only because he thought it belonged to him as of such a family, and valuing himself highly simply because he did not care for Death. This perhaps was a more common feeling than any other. Men were apt to consider themselves very great, and flattered themselves highly, because they possessed that which it was a disgrace not to have, but which a wise man never brought forward but when it was required.

Bishop Jeremy Taylor,[2] in some part of his voluminous works, speaking of a great man, says 'that he was in his ordinary feelings a Coward, as indeed most men are knowing the value of life, but the power of his reason enabled him when necessary to conduct himself with uniform

---

[1] *divided into those*] In 1856 altered to 'divided into two classes', which clarifies the sense; the second class, as Raysor notes, consists of the 'truly Shakespearian characters', like Hamlet and Mercutio, discussed on pp. 77–9.

[2] *Jeremy Taylor*] I have not traced this quotation.

courage and fortitude'. The good Bishop perhaps had in his mind a story
told of one of the ancients. A Philosopher was on board a ship in a storm,
and gave strong marks of fear. A Coxcomb who was on board stepped up
to him, and with the greatest impudence reviled him and said, 'Why are
you so frightened? I am not afraid of being drowned: I don't care a
farthing.' 'You are perfectly in the right,' (replied the Sage), 'your life is
not worth a farthing.'

In all cases Shakespeare never made his characters win your esteem,
but left it to the general command of the passion and poetic justice. It
was most beautiful in the Tragedy of Romeo and Juliet that the great
characters he had principally in view are presumed innocent from all that
could do them injury in our feelings concerning them, and yet the other
characters, which deserve little interest themselves, derive it from being
instrumental in those situations in which the most important personages
develop their thoughts and passions.

Another character of this kind was Capulet: a worthy, noble-minded
old man of high rank, with all the impatience of character which is likely
to accompany it. It is delightful to see the sensibilities of nature always
so exquisitely called forth, as if the Poet had the 100 arms of the Polypus,
thrown out in all directions to catch the predominant feeling. We might
see in Capulet the way in which Anger seizes hold of everything that
comes in its way, as in the lines where Capulet is reproving Tybalt for
his fierceness of behaviour, which led him to wish to insult a Montague
and disturb the merriment:

> Go to, go to,
> You are a saucy boy. Is't so indeed?
> This trick may chance to scathe you—I know what.
> You must contrary me: marry, 'tis time.
> Well said my hearts! You are a princox; go.—
> Be quiet or—More light, more light, for shame!—
> I'll make you quiet: What? Cheerly, my hearts.

The line—'This trick may [chance to] scathe you:—I know what' was
in allusion to the Legacy Tybalt might expect; and then, seeing the lights
burn dimly, Capulet turns his anger against the servants: so that no one
passion is so predominant, but that it always includes all the parts of the
character, so that the reader never had a mere abstract of a passion, as of
anger or ambition, but the whole man was presented; the one predominant passion acting as the leader of the band to the rest.

It would not do to introduce into every piece such characters as
Hamlet: but even in the subordinate personages the passion is made

instinctive at least, even if it has not been an individual, and it has made the reader look with a keener eye into human nature than if it had not been pointed out to us.

It was one of the great advantages of Shakespeare that he availed himself of his psychological genius to develop all the minutiae of the human heart;—that he, shewing us the thing, makes visible what we should otherwise not have seen: just as, after looking at distant objects though a Telescope, when we behold them afterwards with the naked eye, we see them with greater distinctness than we should otherwise have done.

Mercutio was the next character and here begins one of the truly Shakespearian characters, for throughout the Plays of Shakespeare, especially those of the highest order, it is plain that the characters were drawn rather from meditation than from observation, or rather by observation, which was the child of meditation. There was a vast difference between a man going about the world with his Pocket-book, noting down what he hears and observes, and by practice obtains a facility of representing what he has heard and observed—himself frequently unconscious of its bearings. This was entirely different from the observation of that mind which, having formed a theory and a system in its own nature, has remarked all things as examples of the truth, and confirming him in that truth, and above all enabling him to convey the truths of philosophy as mere effects derived from the outward watchings of life.

Hence it was that Shakespeare's favourite characters are full of such lively intellect. Mercutio was a man possessing all the elements of a Poet: high fancy; rapid thoughts; the whole world was, as it were, subject to his law of association: whenever he wished to impress anything, all things became his servants: all things told the same tale, and sound as it were in unison: this was combined with a perfect gentleman, himself unconscious of his powers. It was by his Death contrived to bring about the whole catastrophe of the Play. It endears him to Romeo, and gives to Mercutio's death an importance which it otherwise could not have acquired.

Coleridge mentioned this circumstance in answer to an observation made, he believed, by Dryden, to which Dr. Johnson had fully replied,[1] that Shakespeare had carried on the character of Mercutio as far as he

---

[1] *Dryden . . . replied*] Alluding to Dryden's 'Defence of the Epilogue, or An Essay on the Dramatic Poetry of the Last Age', in *Essays of John Dryden*, ed. W. P. Ker, I, 174. For Johnson's comment, see *The Works of Samuel Johnson*, ed. A. Sherbo, VIII, 956.

could, till his genius was exhausted, and then killed him to get him out of the way. In truth, on the Death of Mercutio the catastrophe depended, and it was produced by it; it served to show how indifference and aversion to activity in Romeo may be overcome, and roused by any deep feeling that is called forth to the most determined actions. Had not Mercutio been made so amiable and so interesting an object to every reader, we could not have felt so strongly as we do the necessity of Romeo's interference, or connecting it so passionately with the future fortunes of the lover and the Mistress.

But what should he say of the Nurse? that, he was told, was the product of mere observation, that it was like Swift's 'polite conversation', which was certainly the most stupendous work of human memory and of unceasingly active attention that exists in human records. The Nurse in Romeo and Juliet was compared sometimes to a Portrait by Gerard Dow, in which every hair was so exquisitely painted that it would bear the test even of the microscope. He appealed to his auditors whether the observation of one or two old nurses would have enabled Shakespeare to draw this character of admirable generalization?—No, surely not: Were any man to attempt to paint in his mind all the qualities that could possibly belong to a nurse, he would find them there. It was an effect produced not by mere observation. The great prerogative of genius (and Shakespeare had felt and availed himself of it) is now to swell itself into the dignity of a god, and now to keep dormant some part of that nature, to descend to the lowest characters; to become anything, in fact, but the vicious.

Thus in the Nurse you had all the garrulity of old age, and all its fondness, which was one of the greatest consolations of humanity. He had often thought what a melancholy world it would be without children, and what an inhuman world without the aged.

You had likewise the arrogance of ignorance, with the pride of real meanness at being connected with a great family; the grossness too, which that situation never removes, though it sometimes suspends, and, arising from that grossness, the little low vices belonging to it, which indeed in their minds were scarcely vices. Romeo at one time was the delightful man, and she was most willing to assist him, but it soon turned in favour of Paris, of whom she professed the same feelings: how admirably too was this contrasted with a young and pure mind educated in other circumstances.

Another circumstance which ought to be mentioned was truly characteristic of the ignorance of the Nurse, which was that in all her recollections she entirely assists herself by a remembrance of visual circumstances. The great difference between the cultivated and un-cultivated mind was this, that the cultivated mind would be found to recall the past by certain regular trains of cause and effect, whereas with the uncultivated it was wholly done by a coincidence of images or cir-cumstances which happened at the same time. This position was exemplified in the following passage which was put into the mouth of the ignorant Nurse. It is found in Act I, Sc. 3, beginning with the lines,

> Even or odd of all the days in the year,
> Come Lammas eve at night she shall be fourteen,

and concluding,

> And since that time it is eleven years,
> For then she could stand alone.

Still going on, added Coleridge, with visual images, which was true to the character. More in fact was brought into one portrait here than any single observation could have given, and nothing incongruous to the whole was introduced.

He honoured and loved the works of Fielding as much, or perhaps more than, those of any other fictitious writer. Take Fielding in his characters of Postilions, landladies, and landlords, or anything that was before his eye, and nothing could be more happy or humorous; but take any of his chief characters, Tom Jones for instance, where the writer was deserted by observation, that where he could not assist himself by his close copying, where it was necessary that something should take place, that some words should be spoken which could not be dictated by mere observation; take his soliloquies, or the interview[1] between Tom Jones and Sophia before the reconciliation, and he would venture to say (loving and honouring the man as he did), that nothing could be more unnatural: words without spirit, wholly incongruous, and without any psychological truth.

But take Shakespeare, and he could ever be found to speak the language of nature. Where did he learn the dialogue of generals? Where was he to have learnt, by observation only, such language as the follow-ing, where Othello is speaking to Iago regarding Brabantio (Act I, Sc. 2)?

> . . . Let him do his spite, etc.

and concluding

> I would not my unhoused free condition
> Put into circumscription and confine
> For the Sea's worth.

---

[1] *interview*] In *Tom Jones*, Bk. XVIII, Ch. 12.

I ask (said the Lecturer), where did Shakespeare observe this? If he did observe it, it was with the inward eye of meditation on his own nature. He became Othello, and spoke therefore as Othello would have spoken.

Another remark he would make on this play was that in it the Poet is not entirely blended with the Dramatist, at least not in that degree which is afterward noticed in Lear, Hamlet, Othello and Macbeth. For instance, Capulet and Montague frequently talked language only belonging to the Poet, and not so much characteristic of passion as of a faculty; a mistake, or rather an indistinctness, which many of our later Poets have carried [through] the whole of their work.

When Coleridge read the song of Deborah, he never supposed that she was a Poet, although he thought the song itself a sublime Poem. It was as simple a dithyrambic Poem as exists, but it was the proper effusion of a woman, highly elevated by triumph, by the natural hatred to oppressors, resulting from a sense of wrongs: it was an exultation on deliverance from them, and this too accomplished by herself. When she commenced,[1]

> I Deborah the mother of Israel,

it was poetry in the highest sense; but he had no reason to suppose that if she had not been agitated by the same passion she would have been able to talk in the same way—or that if she had been placed under different circumstances, which she was not likely to be placed in, she would still have spoken the language of truth.

On the other hand, there was a language which was not descriptive of passion, and yet was poetic and shewed a high and active fancy; as when Capulet says,

> Such comfort as do lusty young men feel,
> When well apparelled April on the heel
> Of limping Winter treads, even such delight
> Among fresh female buds shall you this night
> Inherit at my house.

Other passages more happy in illustrating this might be adduced, where the Poet forgets the character and speaks in his own person.

In other parts Shakespeare's conceits were, in Coleridge's mind, highly justifiable, as belonging to the state of age or passion of the person using them. In other parts, where they could not be so justified, they

---

[1] *she commenced*] The text in Judges V, 7, reads, 'that I Deborah arose, that I arose a mother in Israel'. As Raysor notes, Coleridge was fond of citing the Song of Deborah to illustrate his criticism.

might be excused from the taste of his own and the preceding age; as for instance:

> Here's much to do with hate but more with love:
> Why then, oh brawling love! Oh loving hate!
> Oh anything, of nothing first created!
> Oh heavy lightness! Serious vanity!
> Misshapen Chaos of well-seeming forms!
> Feather of lead! bright smoke, cold fire, sick health!
> Still waking sleep, that is not what it is!

Such passages as these Coleridge dared not declare to be absolutely unnatural, because there is an effort in the mind, when it would describe what it cannot satisfy itself with the description of, to reconcile opposites, and to leave a middle state of mind more strictly appropriate to the imagination than any other when it is hovering between two images: as soon as it is fixed on one it becomes understanding, and when it is waving between them, attaching itself to neither, it is imagination. Such was the fine description of Death in Milton,[1] 'Of Shadow like, but called Substance', etc.

These were the grandest effects, where the imagination was called forth, not to produce a distinct form, but a strong working of the mind still producing what it still repels, and again calling forth what it again negatives, and the result is what the Poet wishes to impress, to substitute a grand feeling of the unimaginable for a mere image. Coleridge sometimes thought that the passage from Milton might be quoted as exhibiting a certain limit between the Poet and the Painter. Sundry painters had not so thought, and had made pictures of the meeting between Satan and Death at Hell Gate, and how was the latter represented? By the most defined thing that could be conceived in nature—A Skeleton, perhaps the *dryest* image that could be discovered, which reduced the mind to a mere state of inactivity and passivity, and compared with which a Square or a triangle was a luxuriant fancy.

After noticing the general and mistaken notion that, because certain forms of writing and combinations of thought were not in common and daily use, they were unnatural, he observed that there was no form of language that might not be introduced by a great Poet with great effect in particular situations, because they were true to nature. And without an original they never could have existed. Take Punning, for instance, which was the most harmless of all kinds of wit, because it never excited

---

[1] *Milton*] The reference is to *Paradise Lost*, II, 669. In the 1856 text Collier quotes the passage.

envy. It might be the necessary consequence of association; as if one man were attempting to show something resisted by another, that other, when agitated by passion, might employ a term used by his adversary in one sense to a directly contrary meaning: it came into his mind to do it one way, and sometimes the best, of replying. It generally arose from a mixture of anger and contempt, which punning was a natural mode of expressing.

It was Coleridge's intention not to pass any of the important conceits in Shakespeare, some of which were introduced in his after productions with great propriety. It would be recollected that at the time this great Poet lived there was an attempt at, and an affectation of, quaintness, which emanated even from the Court, and to which satire had been directed by Osric in Hamlet. Among the Schoolmen of that age nothing was more common than such conceits as he had employed, and it was aided after the restoration of letters, and the bias thus given was very generally felt.

The Lecturer had in his possession a Dictionary of Phrases in which those applied to Love, Hate, Jealousy, and such abstract terms, consisted entirely of phrases taken from Seneca or his imitators, or from the Schoolmen themselves, composed of perpetual antitheses, and describing those passions by conjunction and combination of things absolutely irreconciliable. But he was only palliating Shakespeare as a man, because he did not write for his own but for all ages, and so far he admitted it to be a defect.

If in these lectures we were able to find what were the peculiar faults, as well as the peculiar beauties, of Shakespeare, it would be an additional mode of deciding what authority was to be attached to parts of what were called his works. If we discovered a Play in which there were neither Shakespeare's defects or his excellences, or defects or excellences incompatible with his, or individual scenes so circumstanced, we should have strong reason to believe that it was not Shakespeare's, and that they were taken either from the old plays which, in some instances, he reformed and altered; that they were inserted by some under-hand to please the mob, and that they were written and played because such a part of Shakespeare's original was too heavy, where the mob called for the Clown to lighten the scene. If we found such to be the case, we might conclude that the Play or the Scene was not Shakespeare's.

It remained now for him to speak of the Hero and Heroine of the Play, Romeo and Juliet themselves, and he should do it with unaffected diffidence, not only from the delicacy, but from the great importance of the subject: because it was impossible to defend Shakespeare from the most cruel of all charges against him, viz. that he was an immoral writer, without entering fully into his mode of displaying female characters and Love, which he had done with greater perfection than any other writer, with the single exception perhaps of Milton in his delineation of the character of Eve.

When he heard it said that Shakespeare wrote for man, but the gentler Fletcher for women,[1] it gave him great pain, and when he remembered how much our characters were formed from reading portrayed, he could not deem it a slight subject to [be] passed over as if it were a mere amusement, like a game at Chess. Coleridge could never tame down his mind to think Poetry a Sport or as a[n] amusement for idle hours.

Perhaps there was no one more sure criterion of the degree of refinement in a moral character, and the purity of the intellectual intention, and the deep conviction and sense of what our own nature is in all its combinations, than the different definitions men would give of love, supposing them to be perfectly serious. He would not state the various definitions that had been given; they were probably well known to many, and it would be better not to repeat them. He would rather give one of his own, equally free from extravagance and pretended Platonism, which, like all other things which super-moralize, are sure to demoralize, and yet he had kept it distinct from the grosser opposite.

Considering himself and his fellow men, as it were, a link between heaven and earth as composed of the body and of the soul: to reason, and to will and the perpetual aspiration which tells us that this is ours for a while, but it is not ourselves. Considering man in this twofold character, and yet united in one person, he conceived that there could be no correct definition of love which did not correspond with the being, and with that subordination of one part to another which constitutes our perfection. He would say therefore that,

Love is a perfect desire of the whole being to be united to some thing or some being which is felt necessary to its perfection by the most perfect means that nature permits and reason dictates.

It is inevitable to every noble mind, whether man or woman, to feel itself of itself imperfect and insufficient, not as an animal merely, but altogether as a moral being. How wonderfully therefore has providence provided for us, to make that which is necessary for us a step of that exaltation to a higher and nobler state. The Creator had ordained that one should possess what the other does not, and the union of both is the

---

[1] *Shakespeare . . . women*] See above, p. 74 and n.

most complete ideal of the human character that can be conceived. In everything, blending the similar with the dissimilar is the secret of all pure delight. Who should dare then to stand alone, and vaunt himself in himself sufficient? In Poetry Coleridge had shown that it was the blending of passion with order, and still more in morals, and more than all was it (which woe be to us if we did not at some time contemplate in a moral view solely) the exclusive attachment of the sexes to each other.

It was true that the world and its business might be carried on without marriage, but it is so evident that Providence meant man to be the master of the world; he was the only animal of all climates, and his reason was so pre-eminent over instinct, whose place it supplied, and marriage, or the knitting together of society by the tenderest ties, rendered him able to maintain his superiority over the brutes. Man alone was privileged to clothe himself, and to do all things so as to make him, as it were, a secondary creator of himself, and of his own happiness or misery, and in this, as in all, the image of his Maker was impressed upon him.

Providence then has not left us to Prudence only, for the power of calculation which prudence impels cannot have existed but in a state which pre-supposes the Marriage State. If God has done this, shall we suppose that he has given us no moral sense, no yearning, which is something more than animal, to secure that, without which man might be a herd, but could not be a Society? The very idea seems to breathe absurdity.

From this union arose the filial, maternal, brotherly, and sisterly relations of life, and every State is but a family magnified: all the operations of the mind—all that distinguished us from mere brute animals—arises from the more perfect state of domestic life. One certain criterion in forming an opinion of man was the reverence in which he held woman. Plato had said that by this we rose from sensuality to affection, from affection to love, and from love to pure intellectual delight, and by which we became worthy to conceive that infinite in ourselves without which it were impossible for man to have believed in a God. In short, to sum up all, the most delightful of all promises was expressed to us by this practical state, namely, our marriage with the Redeemer of Mankind.

He might safely appeal to every gentleman in the room whether, when a young man, who had been accustomed to abandon himself to his passions and to have lived with freedom, fell in love, the first symptom is not a complete change in his manners—a contempt and hatred of himself for having asserted that he acted by the dictates of nature, and that they were the inevitable consequences of his youth, and that it was impossible they could be conquered. The surest friend of Chastity is love; it led men not to sink the mind in the body, but to draw the body to the mind, the immortal part of our nature. Contrast this feeling with the works of those writers who have done the direct contrary, even by the ebullitions of comic humour, while in other parts of the same work, from the vile confusion, great purity is displayed, such as the purity of love, which above all other qualities rendered us most lovely.

Love was not like hunger: Love was an associative quality: the hungry savage is a mere animal, thinking of nothing but the satisfaction of his appetite. What was the first effect of love, but to associate the feeling with every object in nature—the trees whisper, the roses exhale their perfumes, the nightingales sing, the very sky seems in unison with the feeling of love: it gives to every object in nature a power of the heart, without which it would indeed be spiritless, a mere dead copy.

Shakespeare had described this passion in various states, and he had begun, as was most natural, with love in the young mind. Did he begin with making Romeo and Juliet in love at the first glimpse, as a common and ordinary thinker would do?—No—he knew what he was about, he was to develop the whole passion, and he takes it in its first elements: that sense of imperfection, that yearning to combine itself with something lovely. Romeo became enamoured of the ideal he formed in his own mind, and then, as it were, christened the first real being as that which he desired. He appeared to be in love with Rosaline, but in truth he was in love only with his own idea. He felt the necessity of being beloved, which no noble mind can be without: Shakespeare then introduces Romeo to Juliet, and makes it not only a violent, but permanent love at first sight, which had been so often ridiculed in Shakespeare.

This called upon Coleridge to remark one characteristic of Shakespeare which he thought belonged truly to a man of profound thought and genius. It had been too much the custom, when we could not explain anything that happened by the few words that were employed to explain everything, we passed it over as beyond our reach; they were looked upon as hints which Philosophy could not explain; as the terra incognita for future discoveries; the great ocean of unknown things to be afterward explored, or as the sacred fragments of a ruined temple, every part of which in itself was beautiful, but the particular relation of which parts was unknown. In Shakespeare they were everywhere introduced with respect, and he had acted upon them, and had drawn his characters as seriously influenced by them.

As he might not again have an opportunity, he would here compare the different manner in which Shakespeare had treated the priestly character, and other writers. In Beaumont and Fletcher they are described as a vulgar mockery; as in other characters, the errors of a few were mistaken for the character of the many, but in Shakespeare they always brought with them your love and respect: he made no abstracts, no copies from the bad parts of human nature; his characters of priests were drawn from the general.

It was remarkable, too, that throughout all his works Shakespeare had never introduced the passion of Avarice. I[t] belonged only to particular parts of our nature: it was only prevalent in particular states of society, and could not be permanent. The Miser of Molière and Plautus was now looked upon as a sort of madman. Elwes[1] was a peculiar individual that partook of insanity, but as a passion it had disappeared, and how admirably did Shakespeare foresee that such characters could not be permanent, in as much as the passion on which they were founded would soon be lost, depending only on accidental circumstances.

None of the Plays of Shakespeare were built upon anything but what was absolutely necessary for our existence, and consequently must be permanent while we continue men. Take the admirable Tragedy of Orestes, or the husband of Jocasta, yet whatever might be the genius of Sophocles, they had a fault. There we see a man oppressed by fate for an action of which he was not morally guilty: the crime is taken from the moral act, and given to the action; we are obliged to say to ourselves that in those days they considered things without reference to the real guilt of the persons.

There was no one character in which Envy was portrayed, excepting in Cassius in Julius Caesar; yet even there it is not hateful to you, but he has counterbalanced it by a number of excellent feelings. He leads the reader to suppose that it is rather something constitutional, something derived from his mother which he cannot avoid: throwing the blame from the will of the man to some unavoidable circumstance, rather than fix the attention of the reader on one of those passions which actually debase the mind.

Wherever love is described as of a serious nature, and much more when it is to lead to a tragical end, it depends on a law of the mind which Coleridge believed he should make intelligible, and which would not only justify Shakespeare, but show an analogy to all his other characters. This subject he reserved to his next lecture.

---

[1] *Elwes*] 'Elves' in MS. The allusion is to John Elwes, a notorious miser, who died, an old man, on 26 November 1789; his story is told in E. Topham, *The Life of Mr. Elwes the Celebrated Miser* (1790).

6

The transcript of Lecture 8

It is impossible, he observed, to pay a higher compliment to Poetry than to consider it in the effects which it has in common with Religion, and distinct, as far as distinct can be, where there is no division, in those qualities which religion exercises, and diffuses over all mankind as far as they are subject to its influence.

He had often thought that Religion (speaking of it only as it accords with Poetry, without reference to its more serious effects) is the Poetry of all mankind, so as both have for their object:

1. To generalize our notions; to prevent men from confining their attention solely or chiefly to their own narrow sphere of action, to their own individualizing circumstances; but by placing them in aweful relations merges the individual man in the whole, and makes it impossible for any one man to think of his future, or of his present lot in reference to a future, without at the same time comprizing all his fellow creatures.

2. That it throws the objects of deepest interest at a distance from us, and thereby not only aids our imagination, but in a most important way subserves the interest of our virtues, for that man is indeed a slave who is a slave to his own senses, and whose mind and imagination cannot carry him beyond the narrow sphere which his hand can touch or even his eye can reach.

3. The grandest point of resemblance: that both have for their object (he knew not whether the English language supplied an appropriate word) the perfecting, the pointing out to us the indefinite improvement of our nature, and fixing our attention upon that. It bids us, while we are sitting in the dark round our little fire, still look at the mountain tops struggling

with the darkness, and which announces that light which shall be common to us all, and in which all individual interests shall dissolve into one common interest, and every man find in another more than a brother.

Such being the case, we need not wonder that it has pleased Providence that the divinest truths of religion should be revealed to us in the form of Poetry, and that at all times the Poets, though not the slaves of any particular sectarian opinions, should have joined to support all those delicate sentiments of the heart (often, when they were most opposite to the reigning philosophy of the day), which might be called the feeding streams of Religion.

Coleridge had heard it said that 'an undevout Astronomer is mad'.[1] In the strict sense of the word, every being capable of understanding must be mad, who remains, as it were, sunk in the ground on which he treads; who, gifted with the divine faculties of indefinite hope and fear, born with them, yet fixes his faith on that in which neither hope or fear have any proper field to display themselves. Much more truly, however, might it be said that an undevout Poet is mad: in other words, an undevout poet in the strict sense of the term is an impossibility. He had heard of *Verse-makers* who introduced their works by such questions as these—Whether the world is made of atoms? Whether [there] is a Universe, or whether there is a governing mind that supported it. These were verse-makers, but it should be recollected that Verse-makers are not Poets. In the Poet was comprehended the man who carries the feelings of childhood into the powers of manhood; who, with a soul unsubdued, unshackled by custom, can contemplate all things with the freshness, with the wonder of a child, and connecting with it the inquisitive powers of his manhood, adds as far as he can find knowledge, admiration, and where knowledge no longer permits admiration, gladly sinks back again into the childlike feeling of devout wonder.

The Poet is not only the man made to solve the riddle of the Universe, but he is also the man who feels where it is not solved, and which continually awakens his feelings, being of the same feeling.[2] What is old and worn out, not in itself, but from the dimness of the intellectual eye brought on by wordly passions, he makes new: he pours upon it the dew that glistens, and blows round us the breeze which cooled us in childhood.

He hoped therefore, that if but in this single lecture he should make some demand on the attention of his hearers to a most important subject,

---

[1] '*an undevout Astronomer is mad*'] Citing Edward Young's *Night Thoughts*, IX, 771.

[2] *and which . . . feeling*] Sic.; in the 1856 text the tangle is resolved by omitting this clause altogether.

upon which mainly depends all the sense of the worthiness or the un-
worthiness of our nature, he should obtain a pardon: if there were less
amusement, he trusted a few thoughts would repay them on after
reflection.

He had been led to these remarks by the Play of Romeo and Juliet, and
some perhaps indiscreet expressions, certainly not well chosen, concerning falling in love at first sight. He had taken one of Shakespeare's
earliest works in order to show that he of all his contemporaries, Sir
Philip Sidney alone excepted, entertained a just conception of the female
character. Certainly that 'Gentleman of Europe', that all-accomplished
man, and our great Shakespeare, were the only writers of that age who
pitched their ideas of female perfections according to the best researches
of philosophy, and compared with all those who followed them they
stood as mighty mountains in a deluge, remaining islands—while all the
rest had been buried by the flood of oblivion.[1]

Coleridge certainly did not mean to justify so foolish a thing, as a
general maxim, as love at first sight: to express himself more accurately,
he should say that there is, and has existed, a feeling, a deep emotion of
the mind, which could only be called *love momentaneous*, not necessarily
love at first sight, nor known by the being himself to be so, but by many
years of after experience. But before[2] he entered into this apparent

---

[1] Collier added a note in 1856 at this point to record that in a later conversation
Coleridge 'made a willing exception in favour of Spenser' (Raysor, II, 149 (113)).

[2] *But before . . . not be quieted*] This passage does not appear in the 1856 text,
where it is replaced by a footnote saying, 'Coleridge here made a reference to,
and cited a passage from, Hooker's "Ecclesiastical Polity"; but my note contains
only a hint regarding it . . .' (Raysor, II, 150 (113)). Collier seems to have noted
down the excerpts from Hooker at the lecture as well as he could, for they are
rather garbled, and possibly include phrases of commentary by Coleridge, so that
it is not clear exactly what the lecturer did quote. Relevant passages from *The
Laws of Ecclesiastical Polity* are the following:
(i) From I, x, 13:
Between man and beasts there is no possibility of social communion, because
the well-spring of that communion is a natural delight which man hath to
transfuse from himself into others, and to receive from others unto himself
especially those things wherein the excellency of his kind doth most consist. The
chiefest instrument of human communion therefore is speech, because thereby
we impart mutually one to another the conceits of our reasonable understanding.
(ii) From I, xi, 4:
For man doth not seem to rest satisfied, either with fruition of that wherewith
his life is preserved, or with performance of such actions as advance him most
deservedly in estimation; but doth further covet, yea oftentimes manifestly
pursue with great sedulity and earnestness, that which cannot stand him in any
stead for vital use; that which exceedeth the reach of sense; yea somewhat above
the capacity of reason, somewhat divine and heavenly, which with hidden
exultation it rather surmiseth than conceiveth; somewhat it seeketh, and what

paradox, he should mention the opinion known throughout Europe by the appellation of the *judicious Hooker*. This venerable theologian and philosopher, far removed from the weak passions of life, and sitting in his closet divining out of his own heart what might be, and feeling the greatness of a future race by the greatness of his own mind, which still permitted him to pursue the noble and the permanent, has told us that,

> The whole spring of all social communion is the natural delight and end which undeprived man appears to transfuse from himself to others, and to receive from others into himself: these things, worn out excellencies of his kind, Death must consist, and the elements of life are the marriage communion, as that this mutual transfusion can take place more perfectly totally, than in any other mode.

The same writer had also stated, in opposition to the materialists, and those who think ignobly of nature, this fact, and has called upon them to answer it consistently with their system:

> Is it not evident throughout life, and attested by all history, that many men have pursued with great sedulity and earnestness that which cannot stand them any need for temporal use; that which exceedeth the reach of their senses, yet somewhat above the capacity of their reason; somewhat divine and heavenly, which, with hidden exaltation, it rather surmiseth than concealeth; somewhat it asketh, and what directly it now hath not; yea, every intimate desire therefore that so interest[s] the mind that all other known delights and pleasures are laid aside; they give place to the search of this: those only I conjecture good, and those I only sought, in obedience to a yearning and a presentiment of their[1]   nature which without that search would not be quieted.[2]

---

that is directly it knoweth not, yet very intentive desire thereof doth so incite it, that all other known delights and pleasures are laid aside, they give place to the search of this but only suspected desire. If the soul of man did serve only to give him being in this life, then things appertaining unto this life would content him, as we see they do other creatures; which creatures enjoying what they live by seek no further, but in this contentation do show a kind of acknowledgement that there is no higher good which doth any way belong unto them. With us it is otherwise. For although the beauties, riches, honours, sciences, virtues, and perfections of all men living, were in the present possession of one; yet somewhat beyond and above all this there would still be sought and earnestly thirsted for.

[1] So MS.; Collier left a space for a word.

[2] *But before . . . not be quieted*] This passage does not appear in the 1856 text.

I have therefore, said Coleridge, to defend the existence of Love as a passion in itself fit for and appropriate to human nature: I say, fit for human nature, and not only so, but peculiar to it; unshared either in degree or kind by any other of our fellow creatures; as a passion which it is impossible for any creature to feel but a being endowed with reason, with the moral sense and with the strong yearnings, which, like all other effects in nature, prophesy some future effect.

If he were to address himself to the Materialists, he continued, and with respect to the human kind (admitting the three great laws which are common to all living beings, viz. the law of self-preservation; that of continuing the race, and that of the preservation of the offspring till protection were not needed), and were to ask him whether he thought that the simple necessity of preserving the race from any motives of prudence or of duty; whether a course of serious reflection, such as if it would be better that we should have a posterity, or if there were any sense of duty impelling us to seek that as our object; if he were to ask a materialist whether such was the real cause of the preservation of the species, he would laugh him to scorn: the materialist would say that nature was too wise to trust any of her great designs to the mere cold calculations of a fallible mortal.

Then the question comes to a short crisis: Is or is not our moral nature a part of the end of Providence? or, are we or are we not beings meant for society? Is that society or is it not meant to be progressive? Not to ask a question which he trusted none of his Auditors would endure; whether, independently of the progression of the race, each individual had it not in his power to be indefinitely progressive? For without marriage, without exclusive attachment, there could be no human society: herds there might be, but society there could not be: there could be none of that delightful intercourse between Father and child: none of the sacred affections, none of the charities of humanity: none of all those many and complex causes which have raised us to the state we have already reached could possibly have had existence. All these effects do not arise among the brutes; they do not arise among those savages whom strange accidents have sunk below the class of human nature, in as much as a stop seems to have been put to their progressiveness.

We may therefore fairly conclude that there is placed within us some element, he might so say, of our nature: something which is as peculiar to our moral nature as any other part can be conceived to be; name it what you will; name it devotion; name it friendship, or a sense of duty: that there is something as peculiar to the moral nature, which answers the moral end, as we find everywhere in the ends of the moral world that there are material and bodily means proportioned to them.

We are born, and it is our nature and lot to be body and mind, but when our hearts leap with joy, on hearing of the victories of our country, or the rescue of the unhappy from the hands of an oppressor, or when a parent was transported at the restoration of a beloved child from a deadly sickness; when the heart beat and the pulse quickened, do we therefore pretend, because the body interprets the emotions of the mind, and, as far as it can, still strives to maintain its claim to sympathy, that therefore joy is not mental? or that joy is not moral? Do we say that it was owing to a particular degree of fullness of blood that our heart leaped and our pulse beat? or do we not rather say that the regent, the mind, being glad, its slave, the body, its willing slave, obeyed it. Or if we are operated upon by a feeling of having done wrong or by a sense of having had a wrong done to us, and it excites the blush of shame, or the glow of anger on our cheek, do we pretend to say that by some accident the blood suffused itself into the veins unusually small, and therefore the guilty seemed ashamed, or the indignant patriot recoiled from a charge against his honour? We scorn it in all these things, and shall it be therefore deemed a sufficient excuse to the materialist to degrade that passion on which not only many of our virtues depend, but upon which the who[le] structure of human society rests, because our body is so united with our mind, that the mind has been employed by Providence to raise what is the lower to the higher: we should be guilty of an act of moral suicide to degrade that which on every account is most noble, by merging it in what is most base: as if an Angel held out the welcoming hand of brotherhood, and we turned away to wallow with the sow in her sty.[1]

The first feeling that would strike a reflecting man, who wished to see mankind not only in an amiable but in a just light, would be that beautiful feeling in the moral world, the brotherly and sisterly affections; the existence of strong affection in the one sex to the other, greatly modified by the difference of sex; made more tender, more graceful, more soothing, and conciliatory, by that circumstance of the difference of sex, yet still remaining perfectly pure, perfectly spiritual, would be a glorious effect of human nature if the instances were only here and

---

[1] *sow in her sty*] In the 1856 text this is changed to 'hog in the mire', and Collier adds a short paragraph, not in the MS., citing the last stanzas of Bk. 2 of Spenser's *Faerie Queene*, including 'Let Grill be Grill, and have his hoggish mind' (Raysor, II, 152 (115)).

there; but how much more glorious when they are so frequent, being only not universal; it is the object of religious veneration to all those who love their fellow men, or who know themselves.

The power of education is herein exemplified, and data for hope are given of yet unrealized excellences perhaps dormant in our nature. When we can see so divine a moral effect spread through all classes, what may we not hope of other excellences of a yet unknown quality ?

By dividing the sisterly and fraternal from the conjugal affections we have in truth two loves; each of them as strong as any affection can be, or ought to be consistently with the performance of our duty and the love we bear to our neighbour. Then, by the former preceding the latter, the latter is rendered more pure, more even, and more constant; the wife has already learnt the discipline of pure love, in the character of a Sister she has already benefited by the discipline of private life, how to yield, how to command, and how to influence. To all this is to be added the beautiful gradations of attachment which distinguishes human nature: from sister to wife, from wife to child, to Uncle, one of our kin, one of our blood, our mere neighbour, our county-man, or our countryman.

The bad effects of this want of variety of orders, this graceful subordination in the character of attachment, Coleridge had often observed in Italy and other countries where the young were kept secluded from their neighbours and families; all closely imprisoned within the same wall till the time when they are let out of their cages, before they have learnt to fly, without experience, aided by no kind feeling, and detesting the control which had kept them from enjoying 'the full hubbub of licence'.[1]

The question is, how has nature and Providence secured these blessings to us ? In this way—that the affections in general become those which urge us to leave the paternal nest. We arrive at a definite time of life, and feel passions which invite us to enter into the world, and that new feeling assuredly coalesces with a new object. Suppose we have a vivid feeling which is new to us: that feeling will more assuredly combine with an external object which is likewise vivid from novelty, than it would do with a familiar one.

To this may be added the variation which seems to have acted very strongly in rude ages concerning anything common to us in the animal creation; likewise the desire to keep up the bond of relationship in families which had emigrated from the patriarchal seed.

---

[1] '*the full hubbub of licence*'] Source untraced. The quotation marks are omitted in the 1856 text.

All these circumstances would render the marriage of brother and sister unfrequent, and this would produce in those simple ages an ominous feeling; some tradition might assist this sentiment or, for ought we know, there might be some law preserved in the Temple of Isis, and from thence obtained by the Patriarchs, from whence arose the horror attached to such connections. This horror once felt, once propagated, the present state of feeling on this subject is easily explained.

Children as early begin to talk of marriage as of death, from attending a wedding or following a funeral: a new young visitor is introduced to the family, and from association they soon think of the conjugal connection. If a child tells his parent that he wishes to marry his sister, he is immediately checked by the stern look, and he is shewn the impossibility of such a union. The lecturer dwelt some minutes on the effect of the stern eye of reproof, not only upon children, but upon persons of mature years. The infant was told that it could not be so, and perhaps the best security of moral feeling arises from a supposed necessity. Thus ignorant persons recoil from the thought of anything because it never has been done, and has been represented as not to be done.

The individual has by this time learnt the greatest and best knowledge of the human mind, that we are in ourselves imperfect, and another truth of perhaps equal importance, that there exists in nature a possibility of uniting two beings, each identified in their nature, but distinguished in their separate qualities, so that each should retain what distinguishes them, and at the same time acquire the qualities of that which is contra-distinguished to them. This is perhaps the most beautiful part of our nature:—the man loses not the manly character; he does not become less brave, or less determined to go through fire and water, were it necessary in consequence of love. Rather say that he becomes far more so. He then begins to feel the beginnings of his moral nature; he then feels the perfectibility of his nature; all the grand and sublime thoughts of a more improved state of being dawn upon him; he can acquire the Patience of woman, which in him becomes fortitude; the beauty of the female character, which in him will become a desire to display what is noble and dignified. In short, he will do what in nature is only done by the blue sky of Heaven; the female will unite the beautiful with the sublime, and the male the sublime with the beautiful.

Shakespeare, throughout the whole of his Plays, has evidently conceived the subject of Love in this dignified light; he has conceived it not only with moral grandeur, but with philosophical penetration. The mind of man searches for some object to assist it in its perfection, which shall assist him, and he also shall give his assistance in completing their moral

nature.[1] These thoughts will occupy many serious moments: imagination will accumulate on imagination, till at length some object shall attract
the notice of his mind, and till at last the whole of the weight of his
feelings shall be directed to this object.

Who shall say this is not Love? Here is system perhaps; here are
associations, here are strong feelings natural to us as men, and they are
attached to one object, and who shall say it is not Love? Assuredly not
the being himself, assuredly no other than he who knows all things.
Shakespeare has therefore described Romeo as in love with Rosaline, and
so completely in love that he declares,

> When the devout religion of mine eye
>   Maintains such falsehood, then turn tears to fires;
> And these, who often drowned, could never die,
>   Transparent heretics, be burnt for liars.
> One fairer than my love? The all-seeing sun
>   Ne'er saw her match since first the world begun.

In this full feeling of confi[dence] Romeo is brought to Capulets, as
it were by accident; he sees Juliet, instantly becomes a heretic, and com-
mences the fulness of attachment which forms the subject of the tragedy.
Surely Shakespeare, the philosopher, the grand Poet who combined
truth with beauty and beauty with truth, never could have dreamed that
it was a mode of interesting the affections of his audience, by making
his Romeo a mere weathercock, who, having seen one woman, became
the victim of melancholy, eating away his own heart; concentring all
his hopes and fears in this form, in an instant changes and falls as madly
in love with another being. Shakespeare surely must have meant something more than this, and Romeo tells us what it was. He says that he had
a different feeling towards Juliet from that he had towards Rosaline. He
adds that Rosaline was the object to which his overbuilt heart attached
itself; that [in] our imperfect nature, in proportion as our ideas are vivid,
they seek after something in which they may appear realized—As men of
genius, conscious of their own weakness, are ready to believe persons
whom they meet the modes of perfection, when in truth they are worse
than themselves: they have formed an ideal in their minds, and they
want to see it realized; they want it something more than shadowy
thought; their own consciousness of imperfection makes it impossible
for them to attach it to themselves, but [in] the first man they meet they

---

[1] The confusion of this sentence is diminished by the rephrasing of it in the
1856 text; see Raysor, II, 155 (118).

only see what is good, and thus have no conjecture of his imperfections, and they fall down, and adore almost, one greatly inferior to themselves.

Such is frequently the case in the friendships of men of genius, and still more frequently in the first loves of ardent feelings and strong imaginations; but still, for a man, having had the experience, without any inward feeling demonstrating the difference, to change one object for another seems without example. But it is perfectly accordant with life: in a life of such various events, such a shifting of scenes, and such a change of personages, we may have mistaken in thinking that he or she was what in truth he or she was not: we may have suffered unnecessary pangs, and have felt idly directed hopes, and then a being may arise who has more resemblance to our ideal: we know that we loved the former with purity, and yet it was not what we now feel; our own mind tells us that the former was but the yearning after the object; in the latter we have found the object correspondent to the idea we had formed.[1]

The same thing arises in every circumstance of taste. What is meant by taste? The inward faculties make a demand. There is a feeling in every man: there is a deviation, and he knows it, between that what is common to all mankind, and that which individualizes him.

---

[1] *formed*] Here the text of the lecture ends in Collier's 1856 version, in which he added a note, 'Here my original notes abruptly break off: the brochure in which I had inserted them was full, and I took another for the conclusion of the lecture, which is unfortunately lost' (Raysor, II, 157 (120)). In the MS., Lecture 8, as printed here, ends on p. 24 of Brochure 7, the remaining 24 pages of which are blank. Lecture 9 begins in Brochure 8.

7

The transcript of Lecture 9

Coleridge's Ninth Lecture

He observed that it is a known and unexplained phenomenon that among the ancients Statuary rose to such a degree of perfection as to leave almost the hope of imitating it baffled, and mingled with despair of excelling it; while Painting, at the same time, notwithstanding the admiration bestowed upon the ancient paintings by Apelles[1] by Pliny and others, had been proved to be an excellence of much later growth, and to have fallen far short of Statuary. He remembered a man, equally admirable for his talents and his rank, [who,] pointing to a sign-post, observed that, had Titian not lived, the richness of representation by colour even there could never have existed. In that mechanical branch of painting, perspective, the ancients were equally deficient, as was proved by the discoveries at Herculaneum and the Palace of Nero,[2] in which such blunders were to be found as to render plausible the assertions of those who maintained that the ancients were wholly ignorant of it. That they were not totally destitute of it is proved by Vitruvius[3] in the introduction to his second book.

[1] *Apelles*] Written out in the short-hand notebook, but omitted from the 1856 text.

[2] *Herculaneum and the Palace of Nero*] Herculaneum, near Naples, destroyed by an eruption of Vesuvius in A.D. 79, was excavated over a long period beginning in 1738; the discoveries there, including some remarkable paintings, were widely reported. Nero's great palace in Rome, the *domus aurea*, was largely demolished by Vespasian, but parts, including some paintings, survive.

[3] *Vitruvius*] Coleridge was perhaps thinking of the preface and first chapter of Bk. 3 of Vitruvius *On Architecture*; or the preface to Bk. 7, para. 11, where a principle of perspective in stage scenery is described.

Something of the same kind appears to have been the case with regard to their dramas. Early in the lectures the Greek stage had been noticed, which had been imitated by the French, and by the writers of England since the reign of Charles II. Their scheme[1] allowed nothing more than a variation of the same note, and admitted nothing of that which is the true principle of life, the attaining of the same end by an infinite variety of means.

It is true that the writings of Shakespeare are not likenesses of the Greek: they are analogies, because by very different means they produce the same end; whereas the greater part of the French Tragedies and the English plays on the same plan cannot be called likenesses, but may be called the failing of the same end by adopting the same means under most unappropriate circumstances.

This had led Coleridge to consider that the ancient drama, meaning the works of Æschylus, Euripides, and Sophocles (for the miserable rhetorical works by the Romans are scarcely to be mentioned as dramatic poems) might be contrasted with the Shakespearian Drama: he had called it Shakespearian, because he knew no other writer who had realized the same idea, although he had been told that the Spanish Poet Calderon[2] had been as successful. The Shakespearian drama might be compared to painting and statuary.[3] In the latter, as in the Greek drama, the characters must be few, because the very essence of statuary was a high degree of abstraction, which would prevent a great many figures from being combined into the same effects. In a grand group of Niobe, or any other ancient heroic subject, how disgusting it would appear were an old nurse introduced. The numbers must be circumscribed, and

[1] *scheme*] In 1856 Collier altered this word to 'theme', adding a note saying he misheard the lecturer and mistakenly wrote 'scheme' in his 'original short-hand note' (Raysor, II, 158 (121)).

[2] *he had been told . . . Calderon*] In his Lecture XII, Schlegel moves from a consideration of Greek tragedy (he mentions Aeschylus and Sophocles), via a slighting reference to Roman drama, to an account of Shakespeare, who is ranked with Calderon as one of the two great modern original dramatists. In the course of this discussion, Schlegel also distinguishes between organic and mechanical form, and compares ancient drama with sculpture, modern drama with painting (*Lectures*, translated Black, II, 92–100; *Vorlesungen*, II, ii, 4–15). The name 'Calderon' is written out in the short-hand notebook, but not 'Lopez de Vega', whose name is added in the corresponding passage in the 1856 text (Raysor, II, 159 (122)).

[3] *painting and statuary*] A comparison developed from Schlegel's Lecture XII; see Black, II, 99–101 (*Vorlesungen*, II, ii, 15–17), 'we compared the antique tragedy to a group in sculpture, . . . the romantic drama must be viewed as a large picture, where not merely figure and motion are exhibited in richer groups, but where even what surrounds the person is also portrayed.'

nothing undignified must be brought into company with what is dignified; no one personage must be brought in but what is abstraction: all must not be presented to the eye, but the effect of multitude must be produced without the introduction of anything discordant.

Compare this group with a picture by Raphael or Titian—where an immense number of figures might be introduced, even a dog, a cat, or a beggar, and from the very circumstance of a less degree of labour and a less degree of abstraction, an effect is produced equally harmonious to the mind, more true to nature, and in all respects but one superior to Statuary; the perfect satisfaction in a thing as a work of art. The man of taste feels satisfied with what, out of his mixed nature, he cannot produce, and to that which the reason conceives possible a momentary reality was given, by the aid of the imagination.

He had before stated the circumstances which permitted Shakespeare to make an alteration so suitable to his age, and so necessitated by the circumstances of the age. Coleridge here repeated what he had before said regarding the distortion of the human voice by the size of the ancient theatres, and the attempt introduced of making everything on the stage appear reality. The difference between an imitation and a likeness is the mixture of a greater number of circumstances of dissimilarity with those of similarity: an imitation differs from a copy precisely as sameness differs from likeness in that sense of the word in which we imply a difference conjoined with that sameness.

Shakespeare had likewise many advantages: the great at that time, instead of throwing round them the Chevaux de frise[1] of mere manners, endeavoured to distinguish themselves by attainments, by energy of thought, and consequent powers of mind. The stage had nothing but curtains for its scenes, and the Actor as well as the author were obliged to appeal to the imagination, and not to the senses, which gave the latter a power over space and time which in the ancient theatre would have been absurd simply because it was contradictory. The advantage is indeed vastly on the side of the modern; he appeals to the imagination, to the reason, and to the noblest powers of the human heart: he is above the iron compulsion of space and time. He appeals to that which we most wish to be when we are most worthy of being, while the ancient dramas bind us down to the meanest part of our nature, and its chief compensation is a simple acquiescence of the mind that what the Poet has represented might possibly have taken place—a poor compliment to a Poet who is to be a creator, to tell him that he has all the excellences of a historian!

---

[1] *Chevaux de frise*] i.e. entanglement.

In dramatic composition, the Unities of Time and Place so narrowed the space of action, and so impoverished[1] the sources of pleasure, that of all the Athenian dramas there is scarcely one which has not fallen into absurdity by aiming at an object and failing, or which has not incurred greater absurdity by bringing events into a space of time in which it is impossible for them to have happened; not to mention that the grandest effort of the Dramatist to be the mirror of life is completely lost.

The limit allowed by the Greeks was twenty-four hours, but we might as well take twenty-four months, because it has already become an object of imagination. The mind is then acted upon by such strong stimulants that the one and the other are indifferent; when once the limit of possibility is passed there are no bounds which can be assigned to imagination. We soon find that such effects may arise from such causes. Above all, in reading Shakespeare, we should first consider in what plays he means to appeal to the reason or imagination, faculties which have no relation to time and place, excepting as in the one case they imply a succession of cause and effect, and as in the other they form a harmonious picture so that the impulse given by reason is carried on by the imagination.

Shakespeare was often spoken of as a Child of Nature, and many had been his imitators, and [they] attempted to copy real incidents, and some of them had not even genius enough to copy nature, but still they produced a sort of phenomenon of modern times, neither tragic, nor comic, nor tragicomic, but the Sentimental. This sort of writing consisted in taking some very affecting incidents, which in its highest excellence only aspired to the genius of an onion, the power of drawing tears, and in which the Author, acting like a Ventriloquist, distributed his own insipidity. Coleridge had seen plays, some translated, and some the growth of our own soil, so well acted and so ill written that, if the auditor could have produced an artificial deafness, he would have been much pleased with the performance as a pantomime.

Shakespeare's characters from Othello or Macbeth down to Dogberry are ideal: they are not the things, but the abstracts of the things which a great mind may take into itself and naturalize to its own heaven. In the character of Dogberry itself some important truths are conveyed, or some admirable allusion is made to some folly reigning at the time, and which the Poet saw must forever reign. The enlightened readers of Shakespeare may be divided into two classes:

1. Those who read with feeling and understanding.

---

[1] *impoverished*] 'impoverishes' in MS.

2. Those who, without affecting to understand or criticize, merely feel and are the recipients of the poet's power.

Between the two no medium could be endured. The reader often feels that some ideal trait of our own is caught, or some nerve has been touched of which we were not before aware, and it is proved that it has been touched by the vibration that we feel, a sort of thrilling, which tells us that we know ourselves the better for it. In the plays of Shakespeare every man sees himself without knowing that he sees himself, as in the phenomena of nature, in the mist of the mountain, a traveller beholds his own figure, but the glory round the head distinguishes it from a mere vulgar copy; or as a man traversing the Brocken in the north of Germany at sunrise, when the glorious beams are shot askance the mountain; he sees before him a figure of gigantic proportions and of such elevated dignity, that he only knows it to be himself by the similarity of action— or as the [Fata Morgana][1] at Messina in which all forms at determined distances are presented in an invisible mist, draped in all the gorgeous colours of prismatic imagination, and with magic harmony uniting them and producing a beautiful whole in the mind of the Spectator.

It is rather humiliating to find that since Shakespeare's time none of our Critics seems to enter into his peculiarities. Coleridge would not dwell on this point, because he intended to devote a lecture more immediately to the prefaces of Pope and Johnson. Some of his contemporaries appear to have understood him, and in a way that does him no small honour: the moderns in their prefaces praise him as a great genius, but when they come to their notes on his plays they treat him like a Schoolboy. Coleridge went on to ridicule the modern commentators still further, asserting that they only exercised the most vulgar of all feeling— that of wonderment. They had maintained that Shakespeare was an irregular poet, that he was now above all praise, and now if possible below contempt, and they reconciled it by saying that he wrote for the mob. No man of genius ever wrote for the mob; he never would consciously write that which was below himself. Careless he might be, or he might write at a time when his better genius did not attend him, but he never wrote anything that he knew would degrade himself. Were it so,

---

[1] *Fata Morgana*] The name by which the mirage-effect Coleridge describes is known; he may have seen it when he visited Messina in 1805. The words are not in the MS., which leaves a blank space, but in the short-hand notebook 'phata Morgana' is written out, confirming that this is what Coleridge said. Collier may have left a blank in the transcription because he did not understand the phrase; it has disappeared from the 1856 text, which simply reads 'near Messina' (Raysor, II, 163 (125)).

as well might a man pride himself of acting the beast, or a Catalani, because she did not feel in a mood to sing, begin to bray.[1]

Yesterday afternoon a friend had left for him a Work by a German writer,[2] of which Coleridge had had time only to read a small part, but what he had read he approved and he should praise the book much more highly, were it not that in truth it would be praising himself, as the sentiments contained in it were so coincident with those Coleridge had expressed at the Royal Institution. It was not a little wonderful that so many ages had elapsed since the time of Shakespeare and that it should remain so for *foreigners* first to feel truly, and to appreciate properly his mighty genius. The solution of this fact must be sought in the history of the nation. The English had become a busy commercial people, and had unquestionably derived from it many advantages moral and physical: we had grown into a mighty nation; one of the giant nations of the world, whom moral superiority still enables to struggle with the other, the evil genius[3] of the Planet.

The German nation on the other hand, unable to act at all, have been driven into speculation; all the feelings have been forced back into the thinking and reasoning mind. To do was impossible for them, but in determining what ought to be done, they perhaps exceeded every people of the globe. Incapable of acting outwardly, they have acted

---

[1] *as well . . . bray*] Angelica Catalani, an Italian soprano, had a great vogue in London after her début there in 1806; Coleridge seems to have dined with her in 1811 (see *The Letters of Charles Lamb*, ed. E. V. Lucas (1935), II, 115). This passage is much changed in the 1856 text, and the reference to Catalani is omitted. Collier added a curious footnote, as if to lend authenticity to his text, which runs as follows (Raysor, II, 164 (126)): 'because Shakespeare could not always be the greatest of poets, was he therefore to condescend to make himself the least ?' In the footnote, Collier adds that his short-hand note reads 'beast' for 'least', but this must be an error, 'the antithesis being between "greatest" and "least", and not between "poet" and "beast" '. See Introduction, p. 17.

[2] *German writer*] In a letter of 6 November 1811, to Henry Crabb Robinson, Coleridge said he was anxious to see a copy of 'Schlegel's Werke', and the *Vorlesungen ueber dramatische Kunst und Litteratur* were presented to him by a German, Bernard Krusve, the day after he delivered Lecture 8 on 12 December; see *Collected Letters*, III, 343, 359–60. Lecture 9 was given on 16 December, so 'Yesterday afternoon' would have been the 15th. The discrepancy in dates is not really significant; it seems clear that Coleridge first read Schlegel on Shakespeare between delivering Lectures 8 and 9 in this series. The *Vorlesungen* were published in three volumes; Vols. I and II, part i, appeared in 1809; vol. II, part ii, was published in 1811. This third volume contains (in the original division of the lectures, changed in later editions), Lectures XII to XV. Lecture XII is on Shakespeare, and Lecture XIII on other English dramatists. Coleridge certainly refers to these two lectures in his own Lecture 9 in December 1811.

[3] *evil genius*] Napoleon (so Raysor).

internally. They first rationally recalled the ancient philosophy; they acted upon their own spirits with an energy of which England produces no parallel since those truly heroic times in body and in soul, the days of Elizabeth.

If all that had been written upon Shakespeare by Englishmen were burnt for want of candles merely to read half of the works of Shakespeare, we should be gainers. Providence had given us the greatest man that ever lived, and had thrown a sop to Envy by giving us the worst critics upon him. His contemporaries were not so insensible: a poem of the highest merit had been addressed to him, and Coleridge knew nowhere, where a more full [description] or contra-distinguishing of great genius could be found than in this Poem.[1] It was as follows:

> A mind reflecting ages past, whose clear
> And equal surface can make things appear
> Distant a thousand years, and represent
> Them in their lively colours just extent
> To outrun hasty Time; retrieve the Fates,
> Roll back the Heavens: blow ope the iron gates
> Of Death and Lethe, where confused lie
> Great heaps of ruinous mortality
> In that deep husky dungeon to discern
> A Royal Ghost from churls; by art to learn
> The [physiognomy] of shades, and give
> Them sudden birth, wondering how [oft they live,]
> What story coldly tells, what Poets feign
> At second hand, and picture without brain,
> [Senseless and soul-less shows: to give a stage
> (Ample and true with life) voice, action, age,
> As Plato's year, and new scene of the world,

---

[1] *Poem*] In the 1856 text, Collier printed the whole of the poem, but in the MS., as printed here, the last thirty-four lines are omitted. Collier also added in 1856 a short paragraph, perhaps his own invention, noting and approving the ascription of the poem to Milton. The full text, first printed in the Second Folio of Shakespeare's plays (1632), together with an account of the controversy over the authorship of it, may be found in the *Shakspere Allusion—Book* (1932), I, 364–8. Schlegel praises the poem as having 'some of the most beautiful and happy lines that ever were applied to any poet' (*Vorlesungen* II, ii, 23; trans. Black, II, 105).

The MS. omits those lines in square brackets. The short-hand notebook contains notes of a few more lines than appear in the MS.; the names 'Clio' and 'Calliope' are written out, and these occur in the five lines following the last line in the MS. I do not know why Collier did not transcribe them in the MS. The text as printed in 1856 was presumably taken by Collier from a printed source.

Them unto us, or to us them had hurl'd:]
To raise our ancient Sovereigns from their hearse,
Make Kings his subjects; by exchanging verse
[Enlive] their pale trunks; that the present age
Joys at their joy, and trembles at their rage:
Yet so to temper passion, that our ears
Take pleasure in their pain, and eyes in tears
Both weep and smile; fearful at plots so sad,
Then laughing at our fear; abus'd, and glad
To be abus'd; affected with that truth
Which we perceive is false, pleas'd in that ruth
At which we start, [and, by elaborate play,
Tortur'd and tickl'd; by a crab-like way
Time past made pastime; and in ugly sort
Disgorging up his ravin for our sport:—
—While the plebeian imp, from lofty throne,
Creates and rules a world, and works upon
Mankind by secret engines; now to move
A chilling pity, then a rigorous love;
To strike up and stroke down, both joy and ire
To steer th'affections; and by heavenly fire
Mold us anew, stol'n from ourselves:—]
This, and much more, which cannot be express'd
But by himself, his tongue and his own breast
Was Shakespeare['s freehold;] which his cunning brain
Improv'd by favour of the nine-fold train.

Never was anything characteristic of Shakespeare more happily expressed.

It is a mistake, Coleridge maintained, to suppose that any of Shakespeare's characters strike us as Portraits. They have the union of reason perceiving and the judgment recording actual facts, and the imagination diffusing over all a magic glory, and while it records the past, [it] projects in a wonderful degree to the future, and makes us feel, however slightly, and see, however dimly, that state of being in which there is neither past nor future, but which is permanent, and is the energy of nature.

Though Coleridge had affirmed, and truly, that all Shakespeare's characters were ideal, yet a just division may be made, [firstly], of those in which the ideal is more prominent to the mind; where it is brought forward more intentionally, where we were made more conscious of the ideal, though in truth they possessed no more or less reality; and secondly, of those which, though equally idealized, the delusion upon the mind is that of their being real. Shakespeare's plays might be separated into those where the real is disguised in the ideal, and those where the ideal is hidden from us in the real. The difference is made by the powers of the mind which the Poet chiefly appeals to.

At present the Lecturer would speak only of those plays where the ideal is predominant, and chiefly for this reason, that those plays had been objected to with the greatest violence; they are objections not the growth of our own Country but the production of France:[1] the judgment of Monkies by some wonderful phenomenon put into the mouths of men. We were told by these creatures that Shakespeare was some wonderful monster in which many heterogeneous components were thrown together, producing a discordant mass of genius and irregularity of gigantic proportions.

Among the ideal Plays was the Tempest, which he would take as an example. Many others might be mentioned but it was impossible to go through every separate piece and what was said on the Tempest would apply to all.—

In this Play Shakespeare has appealed to the imagination, and he constructed a plan according to it: the scheme of his drama did not appeal to any sensuous impression (the word sensuous was authorized by Milton) of time and space, but to the imagination, and it would be recollected that his works were rather recited than acted.

 In the first scene was introduced a mere confusion on board a ship; the lowest characters were brought together with the highest, and with what excellence! A great part of the Genius of Shakespeare consisted of these happy combinations of the highest and lowest, and of the gayest and the saddest. He was not droll in one scene and melancholy in another, but both the one and the other in the same scene: laughter is made to swell the tear of sorrow, and to throw as it were a poetic light upon it, and the tear mixes a tenderness with the laughter that succeeds. In the same scene Shakespeare has shown that power which above all other men he possessed, that of introducing the profoundest sentiments of wisdom just where they would be least expected, and yet where they are truly natural; and the admirable secret of his drama was that the separate speeches do not appear to be produced the one by the former, but to arise out of the peculiar character of the speaker.

---

[1] *France*] Schlegel glances at the objections of 'Frenchmen in particular' to Shakespeare (Black, II, 106–7; *Vorlesungen*, II, ii, 24–5) but in quite different terms from Coleridge here, and without reference to particular plays.

Coleridge here explained the difference between what he called mechanic and organic regularity.[1] In the former the copy must be made as if it had been formed in the same mould with the original. In the latter there is a law which all the parts obey, conforming themselves to the outward symbols and manifestations of the essential principle. He illustrated this distinction by referring to the growth of Trees, which from peculiar circumstances of soil, air, or position, differed in shape even from trees of the same kind, but every man was able to decide at first sight which was an oak, an ash, or a poplar.

This was the case in Shakespeare: he shewed the life and principle of the being, with organic regularity. Thus the Boatswain in the storm, when a sense of danger impressed all, and the bonds of reverence are thrown off, and he gives a loose to his feelings, and thus to the old Counsellor pours forth his vulgar mind:

'Hence! What care these roarers for the name of King? To cabin— Silence! trouble us not.' Gonzalo observes—'Good; yet remember whom thou hast aboard!'

The Boatswain replies, 'None that I more love than myself.—You are a Counsellor; if you can command these elements to silence, and work the peace of the present, we will not handle a rope more; use your authority: if you cannot, give thanks you have lived so long, and make yourself ready in your Cabin for the mischance of the hour, if it so hap— Cheerly good hearts!—Out of our way I say.'

An ordinary dramatist would, after this speech, have introduced Gonzalo moralizing or saying something connected with it; for common dramatists are not men of genius: they connect their ideas by association or logical connection, but the vital writer in a moment transports himself into the very being of each character, and instead of making artificial puppets, he brings the real being before you. Gonzalo replies therefore,

'I have great comfort from this fellow: methinks he hath no drowning mark upon him, his complexion is perfect gallows. Stand fast, good fate, to his hanging; make the rope of his destiny our cable, for our own doth little advantage. If he be not born to be hanged our case is miserable.'

Here is the true sailor, proud of his contempt of danger, and the high feeling of the old man who, instead of condescending to reply to the words addressed to him, turns off and meditates with himself, and draws

---

[1] *mechanic and organic regularity*] Schlegel makes this distinction (Black, II, 94–5; *Vorlesungen*, II, i, 8–9), and observes that we find organic forms 'in nature throughout the whole range of living powers, from the crystallization of salts and minerals to plants and flowers, and from them to the human figure'.

some feeling of comfort to his own mind by trifling with his fate, founding upon it a hope of safety.

Shakespeare had determined to make the plot of this play such as to involve a certain number of low characters, and at the beginning of the piece pitched the note of the whole. It was evidently brought in as a lively mode of telling a story, and the reader is prepared for something to be developed, and in the next scene he brings forward *Prospero and Miranda*.

How was it done ? By first introducing his favourite character Miranda by a sentence which at once expresses the vehemence and violence of the storm, such as it might appear to a witness from the land, and at the same time displays the tenderness of her feelings; the exquisite feelings of a female brought up in a desert, yet with all the advantages of education, all that could be given by a wise, learned, and affectionate father: with all the powers of mind, not weakened by the combats of life, Miranda says—

> Oh, I have suffered
> With those I saw suffer! a brave vessel,
> Which had *no doubt* some noble creatures in her,
> Dashed all to pieces,

The Doubt here expressed could have occurred to no mind but to that of Miranda, who had been bred up with her father and a Monster only: she did not know as others do what sort of creatures were in a ship: they never would have introduced it as a conjecture. This shows that while Shakespeare is displaying his vast excellence he never fails to introduce some touch or other which not only makes characteristic[1] of the peculiar person but combines two things, the person and the circumstances that acted upon the person. She proceeds,

> —Oh, the cry did knock
> Against my very heart—Poor souls, they perished;
> Had I been any God of power, I would
> Have sunk the sea within the earth or ere
> It should the good ship so have swallowed, and
> The freighting souls within her—

Still dwelling on that which was most wanting in her nature: these fellow-creatures, from whom she appeared banished, with only one relict to keep them alive not in her memory but in her imagination.

---

[1] *makes characteristic*] sic; changed to 'is not merely characteristic' in 1856 (Raysor, II, 172 (133)).

Another instance of excellent judgment (for Coleridge was principally speaking of that) was the preparation. Prospero is introduced first in his magic robes, which, with the assistance of his daughter, he removes, and it is the first time the reader knows him as a being possessing supernatural powers. Then he instructs his daughter in the story of their arrival in that Island, and it is done in such a manner that no reader ever[1] conjectures the technical use the poet has made of the relation, viz., informing the audience of the story.

The next step is that Prospero gives warning that he means for particular purposes to lull Miranda to sleep, and thus he exhibits his first and mildest proof of his magical power. It was not as in vulgar plays, where a person is introduced that nobody knows or cares anything about, merely to let the audience into the secret. Prospero then lulls his Daughter asleep, and by the sleep stops the relation at the very moment when it was necessary to break if off in order to excite curiosity, and yet to give the memory and understanding sufficient to carry on the progress of the fable uninterruptedly.

Coleridge could not help here noticing a fine touch of Shakespeare's knowledge of human nature, and generally of the great laws of the mind: he meant Miranda's infant remembrance. Prospero asks her

> —Canst thou remember
> A time before we came unto this cell?
> I do not think thou canst; for then thou wast not
> But three years old.—

Miranda answers

> Certainly sir, I can.

Prospero inquires

> By what?—By any other house or person?
> Of anything the image tell me that
> Hath kept with thy remembrance.

Miranda replies

> 'Tis far off—
> And rather like a dream than an assurance
> That my remembrance warrants. Had I not
> Four or five women once that tended me?

---

[1] *ever*] 'Never' in MS.

This is exquisite.—In general our early remembrances of life arise from vivid colours, especially if we have seen them in motion: persons, when grown up for instance, will remember a bright green door seen when they were young: but in Miranda, who was somewhat older, it was by 4 or 5 women. She might know men from her father, and her remembrance of the past might be worn out by the present object, but women she only knew by herself, the contemplation of her own figure in the fountain, and yet she recalled to her mind what had been. It is not that she saw such and such Grandees, or such and such peeresses, but she remembered to have seen something like a reflection of herself, but it was not herself, and it brought back to her mind what she had seen most like herself: it was a constant yearning of fancy re-producing the past, of what she had only seen in herself, and could only see in herself.

The Picturesque power of Shakespeare, in Coleridge's opinion, of all the poets that ever lived was only equalled by Milton and Dante.[1] The power of genius was not shown in elaborating a picture, of which many specimens were given in Poems of modern date, where the work was so dutchified by minute touches that the reader naturally asked why words and not painting were used? The Lecturer knew a young Lady of much taste who, on reading the recent versifications of voyages and travels that had been published, observed that by a sort of instinct she always cast her eyes on the opposite page for coloured prints.

The power of Poetry is by a single word to produce that energy in the mind as compels the imagination to produce the picture. Thus when Prospero says,

one midnight

Fated to his purpose did Antonio open
The gates of Milan, and i' the dead of darkness
The Ministers for his purpose hurried thence
Me and thy crying self.

Thus, by introducing the simple happy epithet *crying* in the last line, a complete picture is present to the mind, and in this the power of true poetry consists.

Coleridge would next mention the preparation of the reader, first by the storm, as before mentioned. The introduction of all that preceded the tale, as well as the tale itself, served completely to develop the main character and the intention of Prospero. The fact of Miranda being charmed asleep fits us for what goes beyond our ordinary belief, and

---

[1] *Milton and Dante*] So in the 1856 text; in the short-hand notebook there is written out 'Pindar and Dante'.

gradually leads us to the appearance and disclosure of a being gifted with supernatural powers.

Before the introduction of Ariel too, the reader was prepared by what preceded: the moral feeling called forth by the sweet words of Miranda, 'Alack, what trouble was I then to you'—in which she considered only the sufferings and sorrows of her parent; the reader was prepared to exert his imagination for an object so interesting. The Poet made him wish that if supernatural agency were employed, it should be used for a being so lovely.—'The wish was father to the thought'.[1]

In this state of mind was comprehended what is called Poetic Faith, before which our common notions of philosophy give way: This feeling was much stronger than historic faith, in as much as by the former the mind was prepared to exercise it. He made this remark, though somewhat digressive, in order to lead to a future subject of these Lectures, the Poems of Milton.

Many scriptural Poems had been written, with so much of scripture in them, that what was not scripture appeared not to be true: it seemed like mingling lies with the most sacred truths. It was for this reason that Milton has taken as the subject of his work that one point of scripture of which we have the mere fact recorded. A few facts were only necessary, as in the story of King Lear, to put an end to all doubt as to their credibility. It is idle to say then that this or that is improbable because history says that the fact is so. The story on which Milton has founded his Paradise Lost[2] is comprized in the Bible in four or five lines, and the Poet has substituted the faith of the mind to regard as true what would otherwise have appeared absurdity.

Coleridge now returned to the introduction of Ariel, prepared as he had explained. If ever there could be a doubt that Shakespeare was a great Poet acting by Laws arising out of his own nature, and not acting without law as had been asserted, it would be removed by the character of Ariel. The very first words spoken by Ariel introduced him not as an Angel above men, not as a Gnome or a Fiend, but while the Poet gives him all the advantages, all the faculties of reason, he divests him of all moral character, not positively but negatively. In air he lives, from air he derives his being. In air he acts, and all his colours and properties seem to be derived from the clouds. There is nothing in Ariel that cannot be conceived to exist in the atmosphere at sunrise or sunset: hence all

---

[1] *wish . . . thought*] Perhaps Coleridge is recalling *2 Henry IV*, IV, v, 93. The quotation marks were omitted in the 1856 text.

[2] *Paradise Lost*] Altered in 1856 to 'Milton's story'; but 'Lost' is written out in the short-hand notebook.

that belongs to Ariel is all that belongs to the delight the mind can receive from external appearances abstracted from any inborn or purpose.[1] His answers to Prospero are either directly to the question and nothing beyond, or if he expatiates, which he does frequently, it is upon his own delights, and the unnatural situation in which he is placed, though under a good power and employed to good ends. Hence Shakespeare has made his very first demand characteristic of him. He is introduced discontented from his confinement, and being bound to obey anything that he is commanded: we feel it almost unnatural to him, and yet it is delightful that he is so employed. It is as if we were to command one of the winds to blow otherwise than nature dictates, or one of the waves, now sinking away and now rising, to recede before it bursts upon the shore. This is the sort of feeling we experience.

But when Shakespeare contrasts the treatment of Prospero with that of Sycorax, instead of producing curses and discontent, Ariel feels his obligation; he immediately assumes the airy being, with a mind in which, when one feeling is past, not a trace is left behind.

If there be anything in nature from which Shakespeare caught the idea of Ariel [it is] from the child to whom supernatural powers are given; he is neither born of Heaven, nor of earth, but between both: it is like a may blossom kept by the fanning breeze from falling to the ground, suspended in air, and only by violence of compulsion touching the earth. This aversion of the Sylph is kept up through the whole, and Shakespeare, in his admirable judgment, has availed himself of this circumstance to give Ariel an interest in the event, looking forward to that moment when he was to gain his last and only reward, simple liberty.

Another instance of admirable judgment and preparation is the being contrasted with Ariel, Caliban, who is described in such a manner by Prospero as to lead the Reader to expect and look for a monstrous unnatural creature. You do not see Caliban at once—you first hear his voice: it was a sort of preparation, because in nature we do not receive so much disgust from sound as from sight. Still Caliban does not appear, but Ariel enters as a Water Nymph: all the strength of contrast [is] thus acquired, without any of the shock of abruptness, or of the unpleasant feeling which surprise awakes when the object is a being in any way hateful to our senses.

The character of Caliban is wonderfully conceived: he is a sort of

---

[1] *abstracted . . . purpose*] A space for a word is left in the MS. In the 1856 text, this sentence, rather altered, ends with the word 'appearances', and this final phrase is simply omitted.

creature of the earth,[1] partaking of the qualities of the brute, and distinguished from them in two ways: 1. By having mere understanding without moral reason; 2. By not having the instincts which belong to mere animals.—Still Caliban is a noble being: a man in the sense of the imagination, all the images he utters are drawn from nature, and are all highly poetical; they fit in with the images of Ariel: Caliban gives you images from the Earth—Ariel images from the air. Caliban talks of the difficulty of finding fresh water, the situation of Morasses, and other circumstances which the brute instinct not possessing reason could comprehend. No mean image is brought forward, and no mean passion, but animal passions, and the sense of repugnance at being commanded.

The manner in which the Lovers are introduced is equally excellent, and the last point the Lecturer would mention in this wonderful play: in every scene the same judgment might be pointed out, still preparing and still recalling like a lively piece of music. One thing, however, he wished to notice before he concluded, and that was the subject of the Conspiracy against the life of Alonzo, and how our Poet had so well prepared the feelings of his readers for their plot, which was to execute the most detestable of all crimes, and which in another play Shakespeare had called 'the murder of sleep'.[2]

These men at first had no such notion; it was suggested only by the magical sleep cast on Alonzo and Gonzalo: but they are previously introduced as scoffing and scorning at what was said, without any regard to situation or age; without any feelings of admiration of the excellent truths, but giving themselves up entirely to the malignant and unsocial feeling, that of listening to everything that is said, not to understand and to profit by the learning and experience of others, but to find something that may gratify vanity, by making them believe that the person speaking is inferior to themselves.

This was [the] grand characteristic of a villain, and it would be not a presentiment, but an anticipation of Hell, for men to suppose that all mankind was either as wicked as themselves, or might be if they were not too great fools to be so.

It was true that Mr Pope[3] objected to this conspiracy, and yet it would

[1] *Caliban . . . earth*] Schlegel makes the same comment, as Raysor notes: see *Vorlesungen*, II, ii, 129, translated Black, II, 180, 'In the Zephyr-like Ariel the image of air is not to be mistaken . . . as, on the other hand, Caliban signifies the heavy element of earth.'

[2] *'the murder of sleep'*] *Macbeth*, II, ii, 36.

[3] *Pope*] Pope notoriously objected to the long interchange at the opening of II, i, of *The Tempest*, including the satirical comments of Antonio and Sebastian upon Gonzalo, but not to the conspiracy itself.

leave in Coleridge's opinion a complete chasm if it were omitted.

Many, indeed innumerable, beauties might be quoted, particularly the grandeur of the language of Prospero in that divine speech where he takes leave of his magic art, but were he to repeat them, he should pass from the character of a lecturer into a mere reciter. Before he terminated, however, he would take notice of one passage which had fallen under the very severe censure of Pope and Arbuthnot,[1] who had declared it to be a piece of the grossest bombast. It was this,—Prospero addressing himself to his Daughter, directing her attention to Ferdinand:

The fringed curtains of thine eye advance,
And say, what thou seest yond.

Putting this passage as a paraphrase of 'Look what is coming', it certainly did appear ridiculous, and seemed to fall under the rule Coleridge had laid down, that whatever without injury could be translated into a foreign language in simple terms ought to be so in the original or it is not good.

But the different modes of expression, it should be remembered, frequently arose from dif[ference] of situation and education: a blackguard would use very different words to express the same thing, to those a gentleman would employ, and both would be natural and proper: the difference arose from the feeling; the gentleman would speak with all the polished language and regard to his own dignity which belonged to his rank, while the blackguard, who must be considered almost a half-brute, would[2] speak like a half-brute, having respect neither for himself or others.

But Coleridge was content to try this passage by its introduction: How does Prospero introduce it? He has just told Miranda a story which deeply affects her, and afterwards for his own purposes lulled her to sleep, and Shakespeare [makes her] wholly inattentive to the present when she awakes, and dwelling only on the past. The Actress who truly understands the character should have her eyelids sunk down, and living as it were in her dreams. Prospero then sees Ferdinand, and wishes to point him out to his daughter, not only with great but almost scenic solemnity, himself always present to her, and to the spectators as a magician. Something was to appear on a sudden, which was no more expected than we should look for the hero of a Play to be on the stage when the Curtain is drawn up: it is under such circumstances that Prospero says,

[1] *Pope and Arbuthnot*] In the *Art of Sinking in Poetry* (1727), Ch. 12; see the edition by Edna L. Steeves (1952), 69.

[2] *would*] 'And would', MS.

The fringed curtains of thine eye advance,
And say, what thou seest yond.

This solemnity of phraseology was, in Coleridge's opinion, completely in character with Prospero, who was assuming the Magician, whose very art seems to consider all the objects of nature in a mysterious point of view, and who wishes to produce a strong impression on Miranda at the first view of Ferdinand.

It is much easier to find fault with a writer merely by reference to former notions and experience, than to sit down and read him, and to connect the one feeling with the other, and to judge of words and phrases in proportion as they convey those feelings together.

Miranda possessed in herself all the ideal beauties that could be conceived by the greatest Poet, although it was not Coleridge's object so much to point out the high Poetic powers of Shakespeare as his exquisite judgment. But to describe one of the female characters of Shakespeare was almost to describe the whole, for each possessed all the excellences with which they could be invested.

Coleridge concluded by a panegyric upon Shakespeare, whom he declared to be the wonder of the ignorant part of mankind, but much more the wonder of the learned, who, at the same time that he possessed profundity of thought, could be looked upon as no less than a Prophet—Yet at the same time, with all his wonderful powers, making us feel as if we were unconscious of himself and of his mighty abilities; disguising the half-god in the simplicity of a child, or the affection of a dear companion.

8

The transcript of Lecture 12

Coleridge's Twelfth Lecture

In the last lecture he endeavoured, he said, to point out those characters where the pride of intellect, without moral feeling, is supposed to be the ruling impulse, as in Iago, Richard 3rd, and even in Falstaff. In Richard 3rd Ambition was, as it were, the channel in which the reigning impulse directed itself: the character is drawn by the Poet with the greatest fulness and perfection, and he has not only given the character, but actually shown its source and generation. The inferiority of his person made him seek consolation in the superiority of his mind; he had endeavoured to counterbalance his deficiency. This was displayed most beautifully by Shakespeare, who made Richard bring forward his very deformities as a boast. To show that this was not unfounded in nature, Coleridge adduced an anecdote of John Wilkes,[1] who said of himself that even in the Company of ladies the handsomest man ever created had but 10 minutes advantage of him.*—A high compliment to himself, but higher to the female sex.

The Lecturer then proceeded to the Tragedy of Richard 2nd, from its connection with Richard 3rd; as in the last, Shakespeare has painted a man where ambition was only the channel in which the ruling impulse ran, so in the first he has given, under the name of Bolingbroke or Henry

* I am informed that the anecdote was this, by a gentleman who heard him: Wilkes was asked at Fishmongers' Hall how he who was so ugly could boast of his conquest over the fair sex? Wilkes replied that it only took him a week longer.

[1] *John Wilkes*] 1727–97, notorious as a profligate, and member of the 'Hell-fire Club'. The anecdote reported in Collier's note does not appear in the 1856 text.

4th, a character where Ambition conjoined with great talents is the uppermost feeling.

The object of these lectures was to point out the difference between Shakespeare and other dramatists, and no superiority could be more striking than that this great man could take two characters which seem to be the same at first sight, and yet when minutely examined are totally distinct.

The popularity of Richard 2nd was owing in a great measure to the masterly manner in which his characters were portrayed, but were there no other motive, it would deserve it from the fact that it contains the most magnificent and the truest eulogium on our native country which the English language could boast, or which could be found in any other, not excepting the proud claims of Greece and Rome. When Coleridge felt that upon the morality of England depended her safety, and that her morality was supported by our national feelings, he could not read these lines without triumph—When he reflected that, while we were proudly pre-eminent in morals, our enemy only maintained his station by superiority in mechanical means. The passage was as follows: (Act 2, Scene 1) From the words—

This royal throne of Kings, this sceptered isle,

to the words,

Whose rocky [shore] beats back the envious siege
Of Watry Neptune.

Every motive, every cause producing patriotism was here collected without any of those cold abstractions which had been substituted by modern poets. If this sentence were properly repeated, every man would retire from the theatre secure in his country, if secure in his own virtue.

The three principal persons in this play were Richard 2nd, Boling-broke, and York. Coleridge would speak of the last first, as it was the least important. Throughout the keeping was most admirable. York is a man of no strong powers of mind, but of earnest wishes to do right, but contented if in himself alone he have acted well; he points out to Richard the effects of his extravagance, and the dangers by which he is en-compassed, but having so done he is satisfied: there is no future action; he does nothing, but remains passive. When Gaunt is dying he contents himself with giving his opinion to the King, and that done he retires as it were into himself.

As one of the great objects of these lectures was to meet and defeat the popular objections, Coleridge could not here help observing the beauty and true force of nature with which conceits, as they are called, and even sometimes puns,[1] may be introduced. What has become the reigning fault of an age must at some time or other have referred to something beautiful in the human mind, and however conceits may have been misapplied, we should recollect that there never was an abuse without there having previously been a use. Old Gaunt dying sends for the young Prince, and Richard, entering insolently and unfeelingly, says to him

What comfort man? how is't with aged Gaunt?

Gaunt replies

Oh, how that name befits my composition!
Old Gaunt indeed! and *gaunt* in being old:
Within me grief hath kept a tedious fast;
And who abstains from meat that is not *gaunt*?
For sleeping England long time have I watched:
Watching breeds leanness; leanness is all *gaunt*:
The pleasure that some fathers feed upon
Is my strict fast; I mean my children's looks,
And therein fasting thou has[t] made me *gaunt*:
Gaunt am I for the grave: gaunt as a grave,
Whose hollow womb inherits nought but bones.

Richard enquires

Can sick men play so nicely with their names?*

Gaunt answers

No misery makes sport to mock itself;
Since thou dost seek to kill my name in me,
I mock my name, great King, to flatter thee.

Who, said Coleridge, who knows the state of deep passion, must know that it approaches to that state of madness which is not frenzy or delirium, but which models all things to the one reigning idea; still to stray in complaining from the main subject of complaint, and still to return to it again by a sort of irresistible impulse. The abruptness of thought is true

---

* Shakespeare plainly has felt how unnatural this play on words would appear, and makes Gaunt excuse himself or apologize.

---

[1] *puns*] Schlegel defends Shakespeare's use of puns, and refers to 'the affecting play of words of the dying Gaunt' in Lecture XII (*Vorlesungen*, II, ii, 64–6; Black, II, 134–6).

to nature. In a modern poem, called the Mad Mother,[1] she exclaims—

> The Breeze I see is in yon tree,
> It comes to cool my babe and me.

This is an instance of that abruptness of thought so natural to grief, and if it be admired in images, can we say that it is unnatural in words which are in fact a part of our life and existence? In the Scriptures themselves these plays upon words were to be found; as well as in the best works of the ancients, and in the most beautiful parts of Shakespeare, and because this additional grace had been in some instances converted into a deformity, because it had been used in improper places, should we include it in one general censure? When we find it disgusts, we should enquire whether it has been rightly or wrongly used; whether it is in its right or wrong place: it was necessary, in order to form a correct opinion, to consider the state of passion of the person using this play upon words; it might be condemned not because it was a play upon words, but because it was a play in the wrong place. Coleridge felt the importance of these remarks strongly, because by far the greater part of the filth heaped upon Shakespeare originated in this circumstance. Dr Johnson[2] says that Shakespeare loses the world for a toy, and can no more withstand a pun or a play upon words than his Antony could Cleopatra. Shakespeare has gained more admiration by the use of speech in this way than the moderns have acquired by abandoning them: they have in the rules of art lost the admiration, contemplation, and comprehension of nature.

The lecturer proceeded to the character of Richard the Second. He is represented as a man not deficient in immediate courage, as appears by the last assassination,* or in powers of mind, as appears by the foresight he exhibits throughout the play—but still he was weak and womanish, and possessed feelings, which, though amiable in a female, are misplaced in a man, and altogether unfit for a King. In his prosperity he is insolent and presumptuous, but in adversity Dr Johnson says that he was humane and pious;—Coleridge could not assent to the latter epithet, because the same character Richard had shown in the commencement was preserved through the whole. Dr Johnson[3] gave him the virtue

* A man when his life is at stake cannot very well avoid being courageous.

---

[1] *Mad Mother*] Citing ll. 39–40 (reading 'you' for 'the') of Wordsworth's poem so called in *Lyrical Ballads*, but re-titled in 1815, 'Her Eyes are Wild'.

[2] *Dr. Johnson*] In the preface to his Shakespeare; ed. Sherbo, VII, 74.

[3] *Dr. Johnson*] see *Johnson on Shakespeare*, ed. Sherbo, VII, 440; Dr Johnson says Shakespeare gave Richard 'passive fortitude, the virtue of a confessor rather than of a King. In his prosperity we saw him imperious and oppressive, but in his distress he is wise, patient, and pious.'

of a Confessor rather than of a King. It was true, Coleridge admitted, that the first misfortune Richard meets with overwhelmed him, but so far from his feelings being tamed or subdued by it, the very first glance of the sunshine of hope exalts his spirits, and lifts the King into as strange a degree of elevation as before of depression of mind; and the mention of those in his misfortunes who had contributed to his downfall, but who had before been his nearest friends and favourites, calls forth expressions of the bitterest hatred and revenge. Thus, where Richard asks:

> Where is Bagot?
> What is become of Bushy? Where is Green,
> That they have let the dangerous enemy
> Measure our confines with such peaceful steps?
> If we prevail, their heads shall pay for it;
> I warrant they have made peace with Bolingbroke.

Scroop answers:

> Peace have they made with him, indeed, my Lord.

Richard exclaims:

> Oh Villains, Vipers, damned without redemption!
> Dogs easily won to fawn on any man!
> Shakes in my heart's blood warmed, that sting my heart,
> Three Judases each one thrice worse than Judas!
> Would they make peace? Terrible Hell make war
> Upon their spotted souls for this offence.

Scroop adds:

> Sweet love, I see, changing his property
> Turns to the sourest and most deadly hate:—
> Again uncurse their souls: their peace is made
> With heads and not with hands: those whom you curse
> Have felt the worst of death's destroying wound,
> And lie full low, graved in the hollow ground.

On receiving an equivocal answer, 'Peace have they made indeed with him, my Lord', Richard takes it in the worst sense: his promptness to suspect his friends turns his love of them to detestation, and calls forth the most tremendous execrations.

So in the Play, from beginning to end, he pours out all the powers of his mind: he seeks new hope, anticipates new friends, is disappointed, and at length makes a merit of his resignation: he scatters himself into a multitude of images, and in the conclusion endeavours to shelter himself from that which is around him by a cloud of his own thoughts. Throughout his whole character may be noticed the most rapid transitions from insolence to despair, from the heights of love to the agonies of resentment, and from pretended resignation to the bitterest reproaches. The whole is joined with a richness and capaciousness of thought, and, were there an actor capable of representing it, the character of Richard 2nd would delight us more than any other of Shakespeare's masterpieces, with perhaps the single exception of King Lear. Coleridge knew no other character preserved with such unequalled chastity as that of Richard 2nd.

The next character was Henry Bolingbroke, the Rival of Richard 2nd. He appears to be a man of great courage, and of ambition equal to that of Richard 3rd, but the difference between the two was most admirably preserved. In the latter, all that surrounded him was only dear as it fed his inward feeling of superiority; but he was no vulgar tyrant—no Nero or Caligula: he has always an end in view, and a fertility of means to accomplish that end. In the former, that of Bolingbroke, on the contrary, we find a man in the first instance who had been sorely injured; then, encouraged by the grievances of his country and the strange mismanagement of the Government, yet scarcely daring to look at his own views. Coming home under the pretence of claiming his Dukedom, and professing that to be his object almost to the last, but at last letting out his design to the full extent of which he was himself unconscious in the first stages. This is shewn by so many passages that Coleridge would only select one, and he took it the rather because out of 21 octavo volumes of Text and Notes on Shakespeare,[1] the page on which this passage was found was, he believed, the only one left naked by the commentators. It is where Bolingbroke approaches the Castle in which the unfortunate King has taken shelter, and York is in company: the same York who is still contented with saying the truth, but doing nothing for the sake of the truth, drawing back and becoming passive—Northumberland says:

The news is very fair and good my Lord.
Richard not far from hence hath hid his head.

York rebukes him:

---

[1] *21 octavo volumes of . . . Shakespeare*] Coleridge is referring apparently to the edition of 1803 by Isaac Reed, containing the notes of Johnson, Steevens, and Malone. In fact, this page (XI, 101) has several annotations on it, and Coleridge was probably thinking of the speech beginning 'Harry Bolingbroke' cited below, which is on a page (XI, 103) bare of commentary.

> It would beseem the Lord Northumberland
> To say King Richard: alack the heavy day,
> When such a sacred King should hide his head.

Northumberland replies:

> Your Grace mistakes; only to be *brief*
> I left his title out.

York rejoins:

> The time hath been,
> Would you have been so *brief* with him, he would
> Have been so *brief* with you to shorten you,
> For taking so the *head*, the whole *head's* length.

Bolingbroke says:

> *Mistake* not, Uncle, farther than you should.

York replies:

> *Take* not, good cousin, further than you should,
> Lest you *mistake*. The Heavens are o'er your head.[1]

Here the play on words is perfectly in character. The answer is in unison with the tone of the passion, and is connected with some phrase used—Bolingbroke then says:

> I know it, Uncle, and oppose not
> Myself against their will. But who comes here?

And afterwards, addressing himself to Northumberland,

> Noble Lord,
> Go to the rude ribs of that ancient castle;
> Through brazen trumpet send the breath of parle
> Into *his* ruined ears, and thus deliver.

Coleridge had no doubt that the reason Shakespeare used the personal pronoun 'his' was to show that, although Bolingbroke was only speaking of the castle, his thoughts dwelt on Richard the King. In Milton[2] the word *her* was used in relation to *form* in a manner somewhat similar. Bolingbroke had an equivocation in his mind, and was dwelling on the

---

[1] *The heavens are o'er your head*] 'Your head' is the Folio reading, for which Collier substituted in 1856 the Quarto reading 'our heads'.

[2] *Milton*] Alluding to *Paradise Lost*, IX, 457.

King. He goes on, '*Harry of* Bolingbroke'[1] which is almost the only instance in which a name forms the whole line, yet Shakespeare meant it to express Bolingbroke's opinion of his own importance:

> *Harry of* Bolingbroke
> Doth kiss King Richard's hand,
> And sends allegiance and true faith of heart
> To his most royal person, hither come
> Even at his feet to lay my arms and power,
> Provided that my banishment repealed,
> And land restored again, be freely granted:
> If not I'll use the advantage of my power
> And lay the summer's dust with showers [of blood]
> Rained from the wounds of slaughtered Englishmen.

Then Bolingbroke seems to have been checked by the eye of York and proceeds:

> The which, how far off from the mind of Bolingbroke
> It is, such crimson tempest should bedrench
> The fresh green lap of fair King Richard's Land,
> My stooping duty tenderly shall shew.—

Thus checked, Bolingbroke[2] passes suddenly to the very contrary extreme of humility, which would not have been the case had he been allowed to proceed according to the natural flow of the subject. Coleridge also directed attention to this passage, for the same reason:

> Let's march without the noise of threat'ning drum,
> That from the castle's tatter'd battlements
> Our fair appointments may be well perused.
> Methinks, King Richard and myself should meet

---

[1] *Harry of Bolingbroke*] Interlined above this in the MS. is 'Q^re Henry' (i.e. query Henry ?) the word 'of' is also interlined. 'Henry' is again written above '*Harry*' in the first line of the passage quoted. 'Harry Bolingbroke' appears in the short-hand notebook, and in Reed's 1803 edition. The 1856 text reads 'Henry Bolingbroke'.

[2] *Bolingbroke*] Below this in the MS. is written in pencil, 'See short-hand Note A'; the short-hand notebook has a large 'A' on the left opposite a quotation, and below the phrase written out 'eye of Yk'. From this point on, the transcription in the MS. may be of a later date, and it includes one interlined reference to Malone's 1821 edition of Shakespeare (see below, p. 127). However, it also differs considerably from the 1856 text. For discussion of the dating, see above, Introduction, p. 18. In the short-hand notebook, just after note 'A', 'Macbeth' is written out, but this reference does not appear in either the manuscript or the 1856 text.

With no less terror than the elements
Of fire and water, when the thundering shock
Of meeting tears the cloudy cheeks of heaven

When he has proceeded thus far, York again checks him, and Bolingbroke adds:

He be the fire, I'll be the yielding water:
The rage be his, while on the earth I rain
My waters—on the earth and not on him.

Throughout the whole play, with the exception of some of the last scenes; (though they have exquisite beauty) Shakespeare seems to have risen to the summit of excellence in the preservation of character.

The Lecturer then passed to Hamlet, in order, as he said, to obviate some of the general prejudices against Shakespeare in reference to the character of the hero. Much had been objected to, which ought to have been praised, and many beauties of the highest kind had been neglected, because they were somewhat hidden.

The first question was, what did Shakespeare mean when he drew the character of Hamlet? Coleridge's belief was that a poet regarded his story before he began to write in much the same light that a painter looked at his canvas before he began to paint. What was the point to which Shakespeare directed himself? He meant to portray a person in whose view the external world, and all its incidents and objects, were comparatively dim and of no interest in themselves, and which began to interest only when they were reflected in the mirror of his mind. Hamlet beheld external objects in the same way that a man of vivid imagination, who shuts his eyes, sees what has previously made an impression upon his organs.

Shakespeare places him in the most stimulating circumstances that a human being can be placed in: he is the heir apparent of the throne; his father dies suspiciously; his mother excludes him from the throne by marrying his uncle. This was not enough, but the Ghost of the murdered father is introduced to assure the son that he was put to death by his own brother. What is the result? Endless reasoning and urging—perpetual solicitation of the mind to act, but as constant an escape from action—ceaseless reproaches of himself for his sloth, while the whole energy of his resolution passes away in those reproaches. This, too, not from cowardice, for he is made one of the bravest of his time—not from want of forethought or quickness of apprehension, for he sees through the very souls of all who surround him,—but merely from that aversion to action which prevails among such as have a world within themselves.

124

How admirable is the judgment of the poet! Hamlet's own fancy has not conjured up the Ghost of his father; it has been seen by others; he is by them prepared to witness its appearance, and when he does see it he is not brought forward as having long brooded on the subject. The moment before the Ghost enters, Hamlet speaks of other matters in order to relieve the weight on his mind; he speaks of the coldness of the night, and observes that he has not heard the clock strike, adding, in reference to the custom of drinking, that it is

More honour'd in the breach, than the observance.

From the tranquil state of his mind he indulges in moral reflections. Afterwards the Ghost suddenly enters:

Hor.   Look, my lord, it comes.
Ham. Angels and Ministers of grace defend us!

The same thing occurs in *Macbeth*: in the dagger scene, the moment before he sees it, he has his mind drawn to some indifferent matters: thus the appearance has all the effect of abruptness, and the reader is totally divested of the notion that the vision is a figure in the highly wrought imagination.

Here Shakespeare adapts himself to the situation so admirably, and as it were puts himself into the situation, that through poetry, his language is the language of nature: no words, associated with such feelings, can occur to us but those which he has employed, especially the highest, the most august, and the most awful subject that can interest a human being in this sentient world. That this is no mere fancy, Coleridge undertook to show from Shakespeare himself. No character he has drawn could so properly express himself as in the language put into his mouth.

There was no indecision about Hamlet; he knew well what he ought to do, and over and over again he made up his mind to do it: the moment the Players, and the two spies set upon him, have withdrawn, of whom he takes leave with the line, so expressive of his contempt,

Ay so; good bye you.—Now I am alone,

he breaks out into a delirium of rage against himself for neglecting to perform the solemn duty he had undertaken, and contrasts the artificial feelings of the player with his own apparent indifference:

What's Hecuba to him, or he to Hecuba,
That he should weep for her?

Yet the pl⸻ ⸻ weep for her, and was in an agony of grief at her
suff⸻ ⸻ Hamlet could not rouse himself to action that he might
⸻ f his Father, who had come from the grave to incite him

> This is most brave,
> ⸻ ..at I, the son of a dear father murdered,
> Prompted to my revenge by heaven and hell,
> Must, like a whore, unpack my heart with words
> And fall a cursing, like a very drab,
> A scullion.

It is the same feeling, the same conviction of what is his duty, that
makes Hamlet exclaim in a subsequent part of the tragedy:

> How all occasions do inform against me,
> And spur my dull revenge! What is a man,
> If his chief good and market of his time
> *Be but to sleep and feed?* A beast, no more . . .
> . . . I do not know
> Why yet live I to say—'this thing's to do',
> Sith I have cause and will and strength and means
> To do't.

Yet with all this sense of duty, this resolution arising out of conviction, nothing is done: this admirable and consistent character, deeply
acquainted with his own feelings, painting them with such wonderful
power and accuracy, and just as strongly convinced of the fitness of
executing the solemn charge committed to him, still yields to the same
retiring from all reality, which is the result of having what we express by
the term 'a world within himself'.

Such a mind as this is near akin to madness: Dryden has said,[1]
> Great wit to madness, nearly is allied

and he was right; for he means by wit that greatness of genius, which led
Hamlet to the perfect knowledge of his own character, which with all
strength of motive was so weak as to be unable to carry into effect his
most obvious duty.

Still, with all this, he has a sense of imperfectness, which becomes
obvious while he is moralising on the skull in the churchyard: something
is wanted to make it complete—something is deficient, and he is there-

---

[1] *Dryden has said*] 'Great Wits are sure to madness near alli'd', *Absalom and
Achitophel*, 1, 163 (so Raysor).

fore described as attached to Ophelia. His madness is assumed when he discovers that witnesses have been placed behind the arras to listen to what passes, and when the heroine has been thrown in his way as a decoy.

Another objection has been taken by Dr Johnson,[1] and has been treated by him very severely. I refer to the scene in the third act, where Hamlet enters and finds his Uncle praying, and refuses to assail him excepting when he is in the height of his iniquity: to take the King's life at such a moment of repentance and confession, Hamlet declares,

Why this is hire and salary, not revenge.

He therefore forbears, and postpones his Uncle's death until he can take him in some act

That has no relish of salvation in't.

This sentiment Dr Johnson has pronounced to be so atrocious and horrible as to be unfit to be put into the mouth of a human being (See Malone's Shakespeare, vii. 382).[2] The fact is that the determination to allow the King to escape at such a moment was only part of the same irresoluteness of character. Hamlet seizes hold of a pretext for not acting, when he might have acted so effectually. Therefore he again defers the revenge he sought, and declares his resolution to accomplish it at some time

When he is drunk, asleep, or in his rage,
Or in th'incestuous pleasures of his bed.

This, as Coleridge repeated, was merely the excuse Hamlet made to himself for not taking advantage of this particular moment to accomplish his revenge.

Dr Johnson[3] further states that, in the voyage to England, Shakespeare merely followed the novel as he found it, as if he had no other

---

[1] *Dr Johnson*] see *Johnson on Shakespeare*, ed. Sherbo, VIII, 990; Johnson said the speech 'is too horrible to be read or to be uttered'.

[2] The reference in brackets is interlined, and must have been added after 1821, when Malone's edition of Shakespeare in 21 volumes was published. The page reference fits this edition.

[3] *Dr Johnson*] Johnson says nothing of the kind, but a note in Reed's edition of 1803, which Coleridge was apparently using (see above, p. 121 and n.), XVIII, 270, on the speech of Claudius at the end of IV, iii, states 'The circumstances mentioned as including the King to send the prince to England, rather than elsewhere, are likewise found in the *Hystory of Hamblet*.' See also Raysor, II, 197 (154).

motive for adhering to his original; but Shakespeare never followed a novel but where he saw the story contributed to tell or explain some great and general truth inherent in human nature. It was unquestionably an incident in the old story, and there it is used merely as an incident, but Shakespeare saw how it could be applied to his own great purpose, and how it was consistent with the character of Hamlet, that after still resolving, and still refusing, still determining to execute, and still postponing the execution, he should finally give himself up to his destiny, and, in the infirmity of his nature, at last hopelessly place himself in the power and at the mercy of his enemies.

Even after the scene with Osrick, we see Hamlet still indulging in reflection, and thinking little of the new task he has just undertaken; he is all meditation, all resolution as far as words are concerned, but all hesitation and irresolution when called upon to act; so that, resolving to do everything, he in fact does nothing. He is full of purpose, but void of that quality of mind which would lead him at the proper time to carry his purpose into effect.

Anything finer than this conception and working out of a character is merely impossible: Shakespeare wished to impress upon us the truth that action is the great end of existence—that no faculties of intellect, however brilliant, can be considered valuable, or otherwise than as misfortune, if they withdraw us from or render us repugnant to action, and lead us to think and think of doing, until the time had escaped when we ought to have acted. In enforcing this truth, Shakespeare has shown the fulness and force of his powers: all that is amiable and excellent in nature is combined in Hamlet, with the exception of this one quality: he is a man living in meditation, called upon to act by every motive, human and divine, but the great purpose of life [is] defeated by continually resolving to do, yet doing nothing but resolve.

Appendix A

Collier's diary and his reports of Coleridge's conversation in 1856

The passages below are reprinted from the preface to Collier's edition of *Seven Lectures on Shakespeare and Milton* (1856), xiv-l. Most, but not all, of this material was reprinted by T. M. Raysor in *Coleridge's Shakespearean Criticism* (1930), II, 28–55, but he did not include it in the revised version published in the Everyman edition in 1960, so that it is no longer in print. This is the main reason for including it here, for it shows the extent to which Collier, while claiming to be printing the '*ipsissima verba* in my Diary', was in fact rewriting and altering it radically. In the version printed in 1856, he omitted some of the intimate comments on his own state of mind and on his attitude to Coleridge in 1811, changed much in the entries relating to Coleridge, and added material not in the original diary. No doubt he was in Coleridge's company on other occasions than those recorded in the period covered by the diary, from 10 October to 27 November 1811, and perhaps kept other records, as in the diary he refers to a transcript of Coleridge's third lecture written out in some other papers or notebooks. The extent of Collier's omissions, changes, and additions can be seen by comparing what is printed here with the extracts from the manuscript diary on pp. 30–44 above.

It so happens that not one of the persons, whose names are introduced in my Diary, is now alive; and as all I print can do no other injury to their memories than what may arise from my inadequate narration, I may perhaps be permitted to make a few quotations in the words I find written with my own hand about five-and forty years ago. I adopt this course, because I am anxious to preserve all that relates to Coleridge, and to some others, his near friends, into whose company I happened then to fall.[1]

My first note in which Coleridge is mentioned bears date on the 13th October—as I presume 1811; but I am without any guide as to the year, beyond the fact that it appears to have been the 13th October, immediately preceding the 18th November, when Coleridge began his Lectures. My entries are the following:—

'*Sunday, 13th Oct.*—I mentioned, a few pages back, having been in company with Godwin for several hours, and not having heard him say a single word that I cared to remember. Two or three months ago I was in Coleridge's company for the first time: I have seen him on various occasions since, to my great delight and surprise. I was delighted with his gentle manners and unaffected good humour, and especially with his kindness and considerateness for young people: I was surprised by the variety and extent of his knowledge, displayed and enlivened by so much natural eloquence. All he says is without effort, but not unfrequently with a sort of musical hum, and a catching of his breath at the end, and sometimes in the middle, of a sentence, enough to make a slight pause, but not so much as to interrupt the flow of his language. He never disdains to talk on the most familiar topics, if they seem pleasing to others.

'In a conversation at my father's, a little while since, he gave the following character of Falstaff, which I wrote down very soon after it was delivered.

'Falstaff was no coward, but pretended to be one merely for the sake of trying experiments on the credulity of mankind: he was a liar with the same object, and not because he loved falsehood for itself. He was a man of such pre-eminent abilities, as to give him a profound contempt for all those by whom he was usually surrounded, and to lead to a determination on his part, in spite of their fancied superiority, to make them his tools and dupes. He knew, however low he descended, that his own talents would raise him, and extricate him from any difficulty. While he was thought to be the greatest rogue, thief, and liar, he still had that about him which could render him not only respectable, but absolutely necessary to his companions. It was in characters of complete moral depravity, but of first-rate wit and talents, that Shakespeare delighted; and Coleridge instanced Richard the Third, Falstaff, and Iago.

'As Coleridge is a man of genius and knowledge, he seems glad of opportunities of display: being a good talker, he likes to get hold of a

---

[1] *It so happens . . . fall*] Omitted by Raysor.

good listener: he admits it, and told us the anecdote of some very talkative Frenchman, who was introduced to a dumb lady, who, however, politely appeared to hear all her loquacious visitor said. When this visitor afterwards met the friend who had introduced him, he expressed his obligation to that friend for bringing him acquainted with so very agreeable and intelligent a woman, and was astonished and chagrined when he was told that she was dumb![1]

'Coleridge was recently asked his opinion as to the order in which Shakespeare had written his plays? His answer was to this effect, as well as I can remember:—that although Malone had collected a great many external particulars regarding the age of each play, they were all, in Coleridge's mind, much less satisfactory than the knowledge to be obtained from internal evidence. If he were to adopt any theory upon the subject, it would rather be physiological and pathological than chronological. There appeared to be three stages in Shakespeare's genius; it did not seem as if in the outset he thought his ability of a dramatic kind, excepting perhaps as an actor, in which, like many others, he had been somewhat mistaken, though by no means so much as it was the custom to believe.[2] Hence his two poems, "Venus and Adonis", and "Lucrece", both of a narrative character, which must have been written very early: the first, at all events, must have been produced in the country, amid country scenes, sights and employments; but the last had more the air of a city, and of society.

---

[1] *and told . . . dumb!*] Omitted by Raysor.

[2] *believe*] I have a separate note of what Coleridge once said on the subject of the acting powers of Shakespeare, to which I can assign no date, but which I may appropriately add here: it is in these words:

'It is my persuasion—indeed my firm conviction—so firm that nothing can shake it—the rising of Shakespeare's spirit from the grave, modestly confessing his own deficiencies, could not alter my opinion—that Shakespeare, in the best sense of the word, was a very great actor; nothing can exceed the judgment he displays upon that subject. He may not have had the physical advantages of Burbage or Field; but they would never have become what they were without his most able and sagacious instructions; and what would either of them have been without Shakespeare's plays? Great dramatists make great actors. But looking at him merely as a performer, I am certain that he was greater as *Adam*, in "As you Like it", than Burbage, as *Hamlet*, or *Richard the Third*. Think of the scene between him and *Orlando*; and think again, that the actor of that part had to carry the author of that play in his arms! Think of having had Shakespeare in one's arms! It is worth having died two hundred years ago to have heard Shakespeare deliver a single line. He must have been a great actor.'

Here the enthusiasm of the poet may be said to have overwhelmed the sobriety of the critic; for on Sunday, 13th October, Coleridge admitted that Shakespeare had been 'somewhat mistaken' in his own powers as an actor (Collier's note).

'With regard to his dramas, they might easily be placed in groups. "Titus Andronicus" would, in some sort, stand alone, because it was obviously intended to excite vulgar audiences by its scenes of blood and horror—to our ears shocking and disgusting. This was the fashion of plays in Shakespeare's youth; but the taste, if such indeed it were, soon disappeared, as it was sure to do with a man of his character of mind; and then followed, probably, that beautiful love-poem "Romeo and Juliet", and "Love's Labour's Lost", made up entirely of the same passion. These might be succeeded by "All's Well that Ends Well", not an agreeable story, but still full of love; and by "As You Like It", not Shakespeare's invention as to plot, but entirely his own as to dialogue, with all the vivacity of wit, and the elasticity of youth and animal spirits. No man, even in the middle period of life, he thought, could have produced it. "Midsummer Night's Dream" and "Twelfth Night" hardly appeared to belong to the complete maturity of his genius: Shakespeare was then ripening his powers for such works as "Troilus and Cressida", "Coriolanus", "Julius Cæsar", "Cymbeline", and "Othello". Coleridge professed that he could not yet make up his mind to assign a period to "The Merchant of Venice", to "Much Ado about Nothing", nor to "Measure for Measure"; but he was convinced that "Antony and Cleopatra", "Hamlet", "Macbeth", "Lear", "The Tempest", and "The Winter's Tale", were late productions,—especially "The Winter's Tale". These belonged to the third group.

'When asked what he would do with the historical plays, he replied that he was much at a loss. Historical plays had been written and acted before Shakespeare took up those subjects; and there was no doubt whatever that his contributions to the three parts of Henry VI. were very small; indeed he doubted, in opposition to Malone, whether he had had anything to do with the first part of Henry VI.: if he had, it must have been extremely early in his career. "Richard II." and "Richard III."—noble plays, and the finest specimens of their kind—must have preceded the two parts of "Henry IV."; and "Henry VIII." was decidedly a late play. Dramas of this description ought to be treated by themselves; they were neither tragedy nor comedy, and yet at times both. Though far from accurate as to events, in point of character they were the essential truth of history. "Let no man (said Coleridge) blame his son for learning history from Shakespeare." '[1]

---

[1] *Shakespeare*] I have no note of my own of Coleridge's fourth Lecture, but among my mother's papers I met with a memorandum by her (she took the liveliest interest in literary people and literary questions, without the slightest tinge of blue-stockingism) which she had made after that Lecture, from which

I felt that this last sentence was so very applicable to myself, that it will always be impressed upon my mind, and I never shall forget the peculiarly emphatic tone, and rich voice in which Coleridge delivered it. He continued in this strain:—

'He did not agree with some Germans (whom he had heard talk upon the subject) that Shakespeare had had much to do with the doubtful plays imputed to him in the third folio: on the contrary, he was sure that, if he had touched any of them, it was only very lightly and rarely. Being asked whether he included the "Two Noble Kinsmen", among the doubtful plays, he answered, "Decidedly not: there is the clearest internal evidence that Shakespeare importantly aided Fletcher in the composition of it. Parts are most unlike Fletcher, yet most like Shakespeare, while other parts are most like Fletcher, and most un- like Shakespeare. The mad scenes of the Jailor's daughter are coarsely imitated from 'Hamlet': those were by Fletcher, and so very inferior, that I wonder how he could so far condescend. Shakespeare would never have imitated himself at all, much less so badly. There is no finer, or more characteristic dramatic writing than some scenes in 'The Two Noble Kinsmen'." '

The above is what I registered under the date of 13th October, but I find from my Diary that I was again in Coleridge's company at Charles

---

I learn, that in it Coleridge especially treated of the order in which Shakespeare had written his dramas. They there stand thus—

Love's Labour's Lost.	
Romeo and Juliet.	} Youthful Plays.
All's Well that Ends Well.	
Midsummer Night's Dream.	
As you Like it.	
Twelfth Night.	} Manly Plays.
Measure for Measure.	
Much Ado about Nothing.	
Merchant of Venice.	
Troilus and Cressida.	
Cymbeline.	
Macbeth.	
King Lear.	} Mature Plays.
Hamlet.	
Othello.	
Tempest.	
Winter's Tale.	

He proposed to speak of the historical dramas separately, but it is not stated in what order he meant to take them. We see above, that 'As You Like It' he placed among the plays written in manhood, and there is no mention of 'Titus Andronicus', 'The Two Gentlemen of Verona', 'Coriolanus', 'Timon of Athens', 'Julius Caesar', and some others. As above, Coleridge might not intend to enumerate all (Collier's note; omitted by Raysor).

Lamb's on the 16th October, and the next day I wrote as follows:—

'*Thursday, 17th Oct.*—Yesterday, at Lamb's, I met Coleridge again. I expected to see him there, and I made up my mind that I would remember as much as possible of what he said. I went into the apartment, where he and others were assembled, at 8, and before 9 my recollection was so burdened that I was obliged to leave the room for some time, that I might lighten the weight. However, I could not prevail upon myself to stay away long, and returned to the company with a resolution to take the matter more easily. Few others talked, although Hazlitt, Lloyd, Rickman, Dyer, and Burney, with Lamb and his sister, now and then interposed a remark, and gave Coleridge, as it were, a bottom to spin upon: they all seemed disposed to allow him sea-room enough, and he availed himself of it, and, spreading canvas, sailed away majestically. The following is the bare skeleton, and mere bone of what fell from him. He was speaking of Shakespeare when I entered the room:

'He said that Shakespeare was almost the only dramatic poet, who by his characters represented a class, and not an individual: other writers for the stage, and in other respects good ones too, had aimed their satire and ridicule at particular foibles and particular persons, while Shakespeare at one stroke lashed thousands: Shakespeare struck at a crowd; Jonson picked out an especial object for his attack. Coleridge drew a parallel between Shakespeare and a geometrician: the latter, when tracing a circle, had his eye upon the centre as the important point, but included also in his vision a wide circumference; so Shakespeare, while his eye rested upon an individual character, always embraced a wide circumference of others, without diminishing the separate interest he intended to attach to the being he pourtrayed. Othello was a personage of this description; but all Shakespeare's chief characters possessed, in a greater or less degree, this claim to our admiration. He was not a mere painter of portraits, with the dress, features, and peculiarities of the sitter; but a painter of likenesses so true that, although nobody could perhaps say they knew the very person represented, all saw at once that it was faithful, and that it must be a likeness.

'Lamb led Coleridge on to speak of Beaumont and Fletcher: he highly extolled their comedies in many respects, especially for the vivacity of the dialogue, but he contended that their tragedies were liable to grave objections. They always proceeded upon something forced and unnatural; the reader never can reconcile the plot with probability, and sometimes not with possibility. One of their tragedies was founded upon this:—A lady expresses a wish to possess the heart of her lover, terms which that lover understands, all the way through, in a literal sense; and nothing can satisfy him but tearing out his heart, and having it presented to the heroine, in order to secure her affections, after he was past the enjoyment of them. Their comedies, however, were much superior, and at times, and excepting in the generalisation of humour and application, almost rivalled those of Shakespeare. The situations are sometimes so disgusting, and the language so indecent and immoral, that it is impossible to read the plays in private society. The difference in this respect between Shakespeare and Beaumont and Fletcher (speaking of them in their joint capacity) is, that Shakespeare always makes vice odious and virtue admirable, while Beaumont and Fletcher do the very reverse—they ridicule virtue and encourage vice: they pander to the lowest and basest passions of our nature.

'Coleridge afterwards made some remarks upon more modern dramatists, and was especially severe upon Dryden, who could degrade his fine intellect, and debase his noble use of the English language in such plays as "All for Love", and "Sebastian", down to "Limberham", and "The Spanish Friar". He spoke also of Moore's "Gamester", and applauded warmly the acting of Mrs. Siddons. He admitted that the situations were affecting, but maintained that the language of the tragedy was below criticism: it was about upon a par with Kotzebue. It was extremely natural for any one to shed tears at seeing a beautiful woman in the depths of anguish and despair, when she beheld her husband, who had ruined himself by gambling, dying of poison at the very moment he had come into a large fortune, which would have paid all his debts, and enabled him to live in affluence and happiness. "This (said Coleridge) reminds one of the modern termination of 'Romeo and Juliet',—I mean the way in which Garrick, or somebody else, terminated it,—so that Juliet should revive before the death of Romeo, and just in time to be not in time, but to find that he had swallowed a mortal poison. I know that this conclusion is consistent with the old novel upon which the tragedy is founded, but a narrative is one thing and a drama another, and Shakespeare's judgement revolted at such situations on the stage. To be sure they produce tears, and so does a blunt razor shaving the upper lip."

'From hence the conversation diverged to other topics; and Southey's "Curse of Kehama" having been introduced by one of the company, Coleridge admitted that it was a poem of great talent and ingenuity. Being asked whether he could give it no higher praise? he answered, that it did the greatest credit to the abilities of Southey, but that there were two things in it utterly incompatible. From the nature of the story, it was absolutely necessary that the reader should imagine himself enjoying one of the wildest dreams of a poet's fancy; and at the same time it was required of him (which was impossible) that he should believe that the soul of the hero, such as he was depicted, was alive to all the feelings and sympathies of tenderness and affection. The reader was called upon to believe in the possibility of the existence of an almighty man, who had extorted from heaven the power he possessed, and who was detestable for his crimes, and yet who should be capable of all the delicate sensibilities subsisting between parent and child, oppressed, injured, and punished. Such a being was not in human nature. The design and purpose were excellent, namely, to show the superiority of moral to physical power.

'He looked upon "The Curse of Kehama" as a work of great talent, but not of much genius; and he drew the distinction between talent and genius by comparing the first to a watch and the last to an eye: both were beautiful, but one was only a piece of ingenious mechanism, while the other was a production above all art. Talent was a manufacture; genius a gift, that no labour nor study could supply: nobody could make an eye, but anybody, duly instructed, could make a watch. It was suggested by one of the company, that more credit was given to Southey for imagination in that poem than was due to him, since he had derived so much from the extravagances of Hindu mythology. Coleridge replied, that the story was the work of the poet, and that much of the mythology was his also: having invented his tale, Southey wanted to reconcile it with probability, according to some theory or other, and therefore resorted to oriental fiction. He had picked up his mythology from books, as it were by scraps, and had tacked and fitted them together with much skill, and with such additions as his wants and wishes dictated.'

That these were Coleridge's *ipsissima verba* I cannot, at this distance of time, state; but they are the *ipsissima verba* in my Diary; and although I could, of course, take no notes of what passed, I generally wrote down what I had heard, at latest, on the morning after I heard it: so desirous was I of being correct that sometimes, instead of going to rest, I sat up late, and employed myself in putting down brief memoranda, to be extended when I made the entries in my journal.

'The conversation (my Diary continues) then turned upon Walter Scott, whose "Lady of the Lake" has recently been published, and I own that there appeared on the part of Coleridge some disposition, if not to disparage, at least not to recognise the merits of Scott. He professed himself comparatively ignorant of Scott's productions, and stated that "The Lady of the Lake" had been lying upon his table for more than a month, and that he had only been able to get through two divisions of the poem, and had there found many grammatical blunders, and expressions that were not English on this side of the Tweed—nor, indeed, on the other. If (added he) I were called upon to form an opinion of Mr. Scott's poetry, the first thing I should do would be to take away all his names of old castles, which rhyme very prettily, and read very picturesquely; then, I would remove out of the poem all the old armour and weapons; next I would exclude the mention of all nunneries, abbeys, and priories, and I should then see what would be the residuum—how much poetry would remain. At present, having read so little of what he has produced, I can form no competent opinion; but I should then be able to ascertain what was the story or fable (for which I give him full credit, because, I dare say, it is very interesting), what degree of imagination was displayed in narrating it, and how far he was to be admired for propriety and felicity of expression. Of these, at present, others must judge, but I would rather have written one simile by Burns,

> Like snow that falls upon a river,
> A moment white, then gone for ever—

than all the poetry that his countryman Scott—as far as I am yet able to form an estimate—is likely to produce.

'Milton's "Samson Agonistes" being introduced as a topic, Coleridge said, with becoming emphasis, that it was the finest imitation of the ancient Greek drama that ever had been, or ever would be written. One of the company remarked that Steevens (the commentator on Shakespeare) had asserted that "Samson Agonistes" was formed on the model of the ancient Mysteries, the origin of our English drama; upon which Coleridge burst forth with unusual vehemence against Steevens, asserting that he was no more competent to appreciate Shakespeare and Milton, than to form an idea of the grandeur and glory of the seventh heavens. He would require (added Coleridge) a telescope of more than Herschellian power to enable him, with his contracted intellectual vision, to see half a quarter as far: the end of his nose is the utmost extent of that man's ordinary sight, and even then he can not comprehend what he sees.'

So far[1] my note relating to the 16th October, and written on the 17th of that month, but I find that Coleridge was at my father's on the 20th of October, and I have various brief entries of what he said upon several common topics, such as dear and cheap law, military punishments, the state of Ireland, &c. He enlarged upon metaphysics, and expressed his

---

[1] *So far . . . went away.*] Omitted by Raysor.

low opinion of Locke, and his high estimate of the abilities, not of the doctrines, of Spinoza; but as these are matters that I do not well understand now, and had no notion of then, I may be excused for not quoting my imperfect representation. He was peculiarly eloquent (as my note states) on a point to which he was especially led by my father, it being Sunday—the being, benevolence, and attributes of the Creator. I put down what follows immediately after Coleridge went away.[1]

'*Sunday, 20th Oct.*—In religion Coleridge is an enthusiast, and maintains that it must be founded upon moral feeling, and not upon human reason: it must be built upon the passions and sensibilities, and not upon the understandings and intellectual faculties of mankind. Religion was not given to us for any such purpose as the exercise of reason. The moment you begin to reason, that moment you cease to be religious; and on this ground he denied that the Unitarians (to which class he avowed that he formerly belonged) had any religion: they had only a theory. If any person asked him, why he believed in the existence of God, his answer was, because he ought to believe in it, and could not help believing in it; but he would not attempt, as many did, and had done, to prove the being of God. God proved his own existence, and he (Coleridge) gladly believed the evidence. He was strongly inclined to agree with Sir Thomas Browne, in his *Religio Medici*, that religion, in some respects, hardly required enough from our faith. Acknowledging the existence and infinite benevolence of a Creator, he found every feeling of his heart, every pulse of his frame, and every atom in the outer world in harmony with the conviction, and all vibrating to it, like a well-tuned instrument of many strings. He believed in God, because it was inevitable: he would give no other reason, and would seek for no other reason; and he ended by quoting the famous saying of Lord Bacon—"I had rather believe all the fables of the Legend, and of the Talmud, and of the Alcoran, than that this universal frame is without a mind." '[2]

'In the course[3] of the evening Coleridge among other things remarked, no doubt in a great degree fancifully, upon the singular manner in which the number *three* triumphed everywhere and in everything, not to mention irreverently the Trinity—the "three that bear witness in heaven".

Three archangels—Gabriel, Raphael, and Michael.

Three states of being—in heaven, on earth, and in hell.

---

[1] *So far . . . went away.*] Omitted by Raysor.
[2] *Bacon*] Citing the Essay, 'Of Atheism' (so Collier).
[3] *In the course . . . repeated them.*] Omitted by Raysor.

Three religions—natural, revealed, and idolatrous.

Three faiths in Europe—the Christian, the Jewish, and the Mahomedan.

Three great Prophets—Moses, Isaiah, and Christ.

Three lights of the physical world—the sun, the moon, and the stars.

Three natural elements—earth, air, and fire; water being, in fact, only air.

Three colours in nature—blue, yellow, and red; green being in fact, only a mixture of blue and yellow.

Three great ancient empires—the Greek, the Roman, and the Assyrian.

Three forms of government—despotic, republican, and mixed.

Three modern European empires—the Russian, the Austrian, and the French.

Three estates in England—King, Lords, and Commons.

Three Lumina Romanorum—Cicero, Seneca, and Pliny.

Three lumina of the Greeks—Socrates, Plato, and Aristotle.

Three great ancient dramatists—Æschylus, Euripides, and Sophocles.

Three great modern dramatists—Shakespeare, Lopez de Vega, and Goethe.

Three great metaphysicians—Hobbes, Kant, and Hartley.

Three great philosophers—Plato, Aristotle, and Bacon.

Three great ancient historians—Herodotus, Thucydides, and Livy.

Three styles of architecture—Classic, Gothic, and Moorish.

Three great epics—the Iliad, the Inferno, and Paradise Lost.

Three great painters—Raphael, Titian, and Rubens.

Three great sculptors—Praxiteles, Thorwaldsen, and Flaxman.

Three great astronomers—Copernicus, Galileo, and Newton.

Three great satirical characters—by Dryden, Pope, and Churchill.

Three remarkable prose sentences—by Raleigh, Hooker, and Milton.

Three degrees of comparison, three numbers, three genders, &c.

'All these, and some others, which I cannot remember, he enumerated off-hand, and on-hand, for he noted them in succession upon his fingers. He was asked to name the three great satirical characters, and he mentioned either Dryden's Buckingham, or Shaftesbury, Pope's Addison, and Churchill's Fitzpatrick: the three prose sentences were by Raleigh at the close of his "History of the World"; by Hooker in praise of Law, in his "Ecclesiastical Polity"; and by Milton, on the value of good books, in his *Areopagitica*. They were not long, and he repeated them.[1]

---

[1] *In the course ... repeated them.*] Omitted by Raysor.

'He told us that he liked the Odyssey, as a mere story, better than the Iliad: the Odyssey was the oldest, and the finest romance that had ever been written. He could not tolerate the French Telemachus, nor indeed anything that was French, excepting Gresset's *Vert-Vert*, which he had not read for many years. Boileau's *Lutrin* he had never read, but thought his satires pointed and spirited. He would hardly hear of Voltaire as dramatist, philosopher, historian, or novelist. Of the Italians he had the grandest opinion of Dante, but admitted that he was not himself sufficiently master of the language to form a proper estimate. He seemed to have little admiration for Ariosto, and perhaps less for Tasso, but I think he did not know much of them. He had the strongest liking for some of Boccaccio's tales, and spoke in praise of the old English translation of them. Shakespeare had been indebted to several.

'Chapman had translated Homer excellently in some parts, but he did not agree in Lamb's wholesale applause of the verse, and wished that the old poet had continued, as he had begun, in the ten-syllable heroic measure: it would have been more readable, and might have saved us from Pope. Chapman had failed, where he had not succeeded, by endeavouring to write English as Homer had written Greek; Chapman's was Greekified English,—it did not want vigour, or variety, but smoothness and facility. Detached passages could not be improved: they were Homer writing English.'

I have no farther note of what passed on 20th October, nor do I know who was present besides Coleridge. He is the only speaker mentioned, and I dare say that he monopolised the attention of the rest of the company. Such does not seem to have been the case, when what follows passed, in which Wordsworth, Lamb, Hazlitt, and others, had a share of the conversation and the criticism. It appears to be only a part of my memorandum, without date or place, and begins abruptly. I apprehend that the scene must be laid in Lamb's rooms in the Temple, on one of the occasions when Wordsworth was in London, and when people came to meet him.

'Tasso's "Jerusalem Delivered" and Spenser's obligations to Tasso were discussed, and Wordsworth pronounced the Twelfth Canto of the Second Book of the "Fairy Queen" unrivalled in our own, or perhaps in any language, in spite of some pieces of description imitated from the great Italian poets. The allegory, he said, was miraculous and miraculously maintained, yet with the preservation of the liveliest interest in the impersonations of Sir Guyon and the Palmer, as the representatives of virtue and prudence. I collected, however, that Spenser was not in all respects a great favourite with Wordsworth, dealing, as he does so much, in description, and comparatively little in reflection. I may be mistaken, but this was my impression.

'Lamb mentioned the translation of Tasso by Fairfax, of which Wordsworth said he had no copy, and was not well acquainted with it. Lamb gave it as his opinion, that it was the very best, yet the very worst translation in English; and, being asked for an explanation of his apparent paradox, he stammered a little, and then went on, pretty flowingly, to say that it was the best for the air of originality and ease, which marked many of the stanzas, and the worst, as far as he was able to judge, (and he had been told the same by competent Italians) for literalness, and want of adherence to the text. Nothing could be more wanton than Fairfax's deviations, excepting some of those in Sir John Harington's version of Ariosto, into which whole octaves had often been thrust without need or notice.

'Aye, (interposed Hazlitt), that is an evil arising out of original genius undertaking to do unoriginal work; and yet a mere versifier, a man who can string easy rhymes, and employ smooth epithets, is sure to sacrifice the spirit and power of the poet: it is then a transfusion of wine into water, and not of one wine into another, or of water into wine. It is like setting even a tolerable artist to copy after Raphael or Titian: every light and shade, every tone and tint, every form and turn may be closely followed, but still the result is only an unsatisfactory imitation. No painter's own repetitions are equal to his original pictures.

'Miss Lamb adverted to the amazing pains and polishing Fairfax had bestowed upon his work; and a copy of it was produced in which the first stanza, as first printed, and as afterwards altered, were both preserved, one having been pasted over the other. Not only so (said another of the company) but even this emendation did not satisfy Fairfax, for he changed his mind a third time, and had the whole of the first leaf cancelled, in order to introduce a third reading of the first stanza.

'Meanwhile Coleridge had been turning over the pages of the copy produced, and observed that in one place Fairfax had been quite as much indebted to Spenser as to Tasso, and read the subsequent stanzas from Book xvi., with that sort of musical intonation which he always vindicated and practised:—

> The gently budding rose (quoth she) behold,
> That first scant peeping forth with virgin beams,
> Half ope, half shut, her beauties doth upfold
> In their dear leaves, and less seen fairer seems;
> And after spreads them forth more broad and bold,

> Then languisheth, and dies in last extremes,
>> Nor seems the same that decked bed and bower
>> Of many a lady late, and paramour.

> So in the passing of a day doth pass
> The bud and blossom of the life of man,
> Nor e'er doth flourish more, but, like the grass
> Cut down, becometh wither'd pale and wan.
> O! gather then the rose while time thou has;
> Short is the day, done when it scant began,
>> Gather the rose of love, while yet thou may'st
>> Loving be lov'd, embracing be embrac'd.

'Nobody was prepared to say, from memory, how far the above was or was not a literal rendering of Tasso's original; but nobody doubted that it was very like Spenser, in the Canto which Wordsworth had not long before so warmly praised. Coleridge repeated, with a very little prompting, the following stanza from Book ii. c. 12, of the "Fairy Queen", for the purpose of proving how closely Fairfax had followed Spenser.

> So passeth, in the passing of a day,
>> Of mortal life the leaf, the bud, the flower,
>> Ne more doth flourish after first decay,
>> That erst was sought to deck both bed and bower
>> Of many a lady, and many a paramour.
> Gather therefore the rose whilst yet is prime,
> For soon comes age that will her pride deflower:
> Gather the rose of love, whilst yet is time,
>> Whilst loving thou may'st loved be with equal crime.

'It was held, on all hands, sufficiently established, that Fairfax, in translating Tasso, must have had Spenser in his memory, if not in his eye; and it was contended by Hazlitt, that it would have been impossible for Fairfax to have done better: moreover, he insisted that in translating this part of the *Gerusalemme Liberata*, he could not have acquitted himself at all adequately, without approaching so near Spenser as absolutely to tread upon his heels. "But, (added Lamb stuttering) he has not only trodden upon his heels, but upon his toes too: I hope he had neither kibes nor corns."

'Lamb, I think it was, remarked upon the circumstance that Spenser, in the last line of the stanza quoted, had not, as in many other instances, observed the cæsura in the closing Alexandrine, so that the line could not be read musically without dividing "lovéd" into two syllables. It was Southey's opinion, somebody said, that the Alexandrine could never be written and read properly without that pause. Wordsworth took the contrary side, and repeated several twelve-syllable lines of his own, where there could be no pause after the sixth syllable: I only remember one of his examples:—

And near a thousand tables pined, and wanted food,

from a poem he had called "The Female Vagrant":[1] here "tables" must have a cæsura after the first syllable, if at all. I think he said that the poem was not yet printed, but I am not sure on that point.'

My next note with a date is the 1st November, but without the day of the week, and perhaps it was the day of which I made my minute. Again I saw Coleridge, and again I was an attentive listener. He once more quoted his favourite simile from Burns, in order to establish the position, that one of the purposes and tests of true poetry was the employment of common objects in uncommon ways—the felicitous and novel use of images of daily occurrence. Everybody had seen snow falling upon a river, and vanishing instantly, but who had applied this result of ordinary experience with such novelty and beauty? My note goes on thus, under the date of—

'*1st November.*—"Shakespeare," said Coleridge, "is full of these familiar images and illustrations: Milton has them too, but they do not occur so frequently, because his subject does not so naturally call for them. He is the truest poet who can apply to a new purpose the oldest occurrences, and most usual appearances: the justice of the images can then always be felt and appreciated."

'Adverting to his contemporaries, he told us that, of course, he knew nearly every line Southey had written, but he repeated that he was far from well read in Scott, whom he now said he personally liked, adding that he had just finished Campbell's "Gertrude of Wyoming": though personally he did not much relish the author, he admitted that his poem contained very pretty stanzas. He disclaimed all envy: each of the three had met with more success than he should ever arrive at; but that success was quite as much owing to their faults as to their excellences. He did not generally like to speak of his contemporaries, but if he did speak of them, he must give his fair opinion, and that opinion was, that not one of the three—neither Southey, Scott, nor Campbell—would by

---

[1] *The Female Vagrant*] Citing l. 144 of the poem so-called in *Lyrical Ballads*, l. 369 of the revised version, 'Guilt and Sorrow'.

their poetry survive much beyond the day when they lived and wrote. Their works seemed to him not to have the seeds of vitality, the real germs of long life. The two first were entertaining as tellers of stories in verse; but the last in his "Pleasures of Hope" obviously had no fixed design, but when a thought (of course, not a very original one) came into his head, he put it down in couplets, and afterwards strung the *disjecta membra* (not *poetæ*) together. Some of the best things in it were borrowed: for instance, the line—

> And Freedom shriek'd when Kosciusko fell

was taken from a much ridiculed piece by Dennis,[1] a pindaric on William III.,

> Fair Liberty shriek'd out aloud, aloud Religion groan'd.

It is the same production in which the following much-laughed-at specimen of bathos is found:

> Nor Alps nor Pyrenneans keep him out,
> Nor fortified redoubt.

Coleridge had little toleration for Campbell, and considered him, as far as he had gone, a mere verse-maker. Southey was, in some sort, like an elegant setter of jewels; the stones were not his own: he gave them all the advantage of his art—the charm of his workmanship (and that charm was great), but not their native brilliancy. Wordsworth was not popular, and never would be so, for this reason among others—that he was a better poet than the rest. Yet Wordsworth liked popularity, and would fain be popular, if he could.

' "For my part (said Coleridge) I freely own that I have no title to the name of a poet, according to my own definition of poetry. (He did not state his definition.) Many years ago a small volume of verses came out with my name: it was not my doing, but Cottle offered me £20, when I much wanted it, for some short pieces I had written at Cambridge, and I sold the manuscripts to him, but I declare that I had no notion, at the time, that they were meant for publication; my poverty, and not my will, consented. Cottle paid my poverty, and I was dubbed poet, almost before I knew whether I was in Bristol or in London. I met people in the streets who congratulated me upon being a poet, and that was the first

---

[1] *Dennis*] 'A Pindarick Ode on the King. Written in the beginning of August 1691, occasion'd by the Victory at Aghrim.' In the first line cited, 'when' should read 'as', and in the third quotation, 'keep him out' should read 'keep it out' (so Raysor).

notice I had of my new rank and dignity. I was to have had £20 for what Cottle bought, but I never received more than £15, and for this paltry sum I was styled poet by the reviewers, who fell foul of me for what they termed my bombast and buckram. Nevertheless 500 copies were sold, and a new edition being called for, I pleaded guilty to the charge of inflation and grandiloquence. But now, only see the contrast! Wordsworth has printed two poems of mine, but without my name, and again the reviewers have laid their claws upon me, and for what? Not for bombast and buckram—not for inflation and grandiloquence, but for mock simplicity; and now I am put down as the master of a school for the instruction of grown children in nursery rhymes." '

It then appears[1] from my Diary, under the same date, that Coleridge recited portions (only portions, for his memory did not serve him for the whole) of the celebrated satirical piece called 'The Devil's Walk'. I distinctly understood him to claim the composition of it, excepting in one or two places, where he had been assisted by Southey, and, I am pretty sure that he added, by Lamb. I only notice this point because in the course of my life I have heard 'The Devil's Walk' attributed to at least half-a-dozen other people, among others to Sir E. Bulwer Lytton, who, I believe, was not born at the time it was perpetrated. My journal proceeds in these terms:—

'6 *November.*—Some short time ago Coleridge lent me a manuscript copy of "Christabel". He told us that the earlier portion of it was written before he went to Germany; but it has, in some respects, a German air. I informed him that I had a manuscript of it already, made some years before by a lady of Salisbury; but he said that he had materially altered it in several places from his first draught, especially in the first part, and I borrowed his copy for the purpose of comparison. I showed him my copy, and he recognised the hand-writing. I here note some of the recent alterations, which are generally for the better. The line in my copy, near the beginning,

> The breezes they were still also,

he has changed in his copy to

> The breezes they were whispering low:

probably he did not like "also" for a rhyme.[2]

---

[1] *It then appears . . . saw him*] Omitted by Raysor.

[2] *rhyme*] He gave me a printed copy when Christabel first came out, I think in 1816: it had his autograph and a few words on the title-page, but I have in some unaccountable way lost it. I observe that this line

> The breezes they were whispering low,

'Coleridge himself pointed out to me the subsequent blunder in my Salisbury copy, where the poet speaks of the ornaments in the hair of Christabel,

> And the jewels were *tumbled* in her hair:

It ought to have been, as he had written it,

> And the jewels were tangled in her hair.[1]

In my Salisbury MS., Geraldine is made to say,

> Five ruffians seiz'd me yestermorn,

and Coleridge substituted *warriors* for "ruffians". He has also improved the line,

> For I have lain in fits, I wis,

to this form,

> For I have lain entranc'd, I wis.

In my Salisbury MS. there is this passage:

> Her lucky stars the lady blest,
> And Christabel she sweetly said,
> All our household are at rest,
> Each one sleeping in his bed.

In Coleridge's copy it stands,

> Her smiling stars the lady blest,
> And thus bespake sweet Christabel:
> All our household is at rest,
> The hall as silent as a cell.[2]

---

is altogether changed in Pickering's edition of Coleridge's Poetical Works, 1847, 12mo, vol. ii. p. 30, where it stands
> The sighs she heav'd were soft and low;
but sighs could hardly be otherwise than 'soft and low' (Collier's note).

[1] Here again the printed copy of 1847 differs slightly from my Salisbury copy, and from that which Coleridge lent me: it runs,
> The *gems entangled* in her hair
(Collier's note).

[2] In Pickering's edition of 1847 the epithet to 'stars' is neither 'lucky' nor 'smiling', but *gracious*, so fastidious was Coleridge. In the next line, for 'thus bespake', we read 'thus *spake on*'; and for 'silent as a cell', we have 'silent as *the* cell' (Collier's note).

'My Salisbury copy omits a very necessary line,

> And Christabel saw the lady's eye,

which Coleridge observed, and observed upon, saying that

> And nothing else she saw thereby

had consequently no corresponding rhyme; besides, unless Christabel had seen "the lady's eye", it would be difficult to account for the subsequent state of the heroine's mind. There is an alteration in the copy which Coleridge lent me, merely of an epithet, which I cannot approve: it is where Christabel says, in my Salisbury MS.,

> O, weary lady Geraldine,
> I pray you drink this spicy wine.

'Wine, of old, was often spiced, but Coleridge, by his alteration, loses this touch of antiquity, and represents Geraldine as taking a cordial:

> I pray you drink this *cordial* wine.

'Then, in my Salisbury MS., follows a couplet, very much in the monthly-nurse style;

> Nay, drink it up; I pray you do:
> Believe me, it will comfort you.

'These Coleridge has judiciously struck entirely out in his copy. In the same sick-room strain Geraldine is represented, in my Salisbury copy, as saying, after she has taken the "spicy wine", "I'm better now", but Coleridge discreetly amends the couplet thus:

> The lady wip'd her moist cold brow,
> And faintly said, '*Tis over now.*

'These variations are only in the first part of the poem: the second part was written after a considerable interval, and there the differences, between my Salisbury copy and that which the author has placed in my hands, are insignificant; chiefly verbal: thus

> The vision foul of fear and pain,

is made to run

> The vision of fear, the touch of pain.

'Afterwards, for what in my Salisbury copy is

> The pang, the sight was past away,

Coleridge writes

> The touch, the sight had pass'd away.

'Both copies end as follows:

> The aged knight Sir Leoline
> Led forth the Lady Geraldine.

The preceding is the whole of my memorandum regarding 'Christabel', certainly the most popular of Coleridge's productions; and as nothing is said of any 'Conclusion to Part II.', as it appears in Pickering's edition of 1847, I presume that it was not appended to the MS. lent to me by the author. Unquestionably, there is nothing of the kind in my Salisbury MS. I returned Coleridge's copy, probably the next time I saw him.[1]

I cannot pretend to explain it, but there has been some dislocation and derangement of my Diary about this period. The dates are sometimes not given at all; and here, after 'Nov. 6', follows an entry of 'Oct. 29th'. During the many years when my MSS. were lost, they seem to have been subjected to much ill-treatment, and instead of regretting that they have been mangled, I ought perhaps to rejoice that any of them have been preserved. This remark especially applies to what follows, which occurs, as I said, under

'*29th October*.—Coleridge told us (though I fancy, from his indecision of character, that it may turn out a mere project—I hope not) that he means very soon to give a series of lectures at Coachmakers' Hall, mainly upon Poetry, with a view to erect some standard by which all writers of verse may be measured and ranked. He added, that many of his friends had advised him to take this step, and for his own part he was not at all unwilling to comply with their wishes. His lectures would, necessarily, embrace criticisms on Shakespeare, Milton, and all the chief and most popular poets of our language, from Chaucer, for whom he had great reverence, down to Campbell, for whom he had little admiration. He thought that something of the kind was much needed, in order to settle people's notions as to what was, or was not good poetry, and who was, or was not a good poet. He talked of carrying out this scheme next month.

'He mentioned, as indeed we knew, that last year he had delivered Lectures upon Poetry at the Royal Institution: for the first of the series he had prepared himself fully, and when it was over he received many

---

[1] *It then appears . . . saw him*] Omitted by Raysor.

high-flown, but frigid compliments, evidently, like his lecture, studied. For the second lecture he had prepared himself less elaborately, and was much applauded. For the third lecture, and indeed for the remainder of the course, he made no preparation, and was liked better than ever, and vociferously and heartily cheered. The reason was obvious, for what came warm from the heart of the speaker, went warm to the heart of the hearer; and although the illustrations might not be so good, yet being extemporaneous, and often from objects immediately before the eyes, they made more impression, and seemed to have more aptitude.'

These promised lectures at Coachmakers' Hall, spoken of in the beginning of the preceding extract, were in fact delivered at the Scot's Corporation Hall, and began on the 18th Nov., 1811: notes of[1] seven out of fifteen of them follow this Preface. If ever, by some remote chance, I recover the missing portions of my Diary—if they have not all been irrecoverably lost or destroyed—I shall find there various other notices respecting Coleridge and some of his friends, doubtless with the precise dates belonging to them. The few remaining memoranda of conversations in which he engaged are upon separate papers, and some of them are without day or year. The following is well worth preservation, and must have passed about the same period as the foregoing:—

'We talked of dreams, the subject having been introduced by a recitation by Coleridge of some lines he had written many years ago upon the building of a Dream-palace by Kubla-Khan: he had founded it on a passage he had met with in an old book of travels. Lamb maintained that the most impressive dream he had ever read was Clarence's, in "Richard III.", which was not now allowed to form part of the acted play. There was another famous dream in Shakespeare, that of Antigonus in the "Winter's Tale", and all illustrated the line in Spenser's "Fairy Queen", Book iv. c. 5:

The things which day most minds at night do most appear;

the truth of which every body's experience proved, and therefore every body at once acknowledged. Coleridge observed that there was something quite as true, near the same place in the poem, which was not unlikely to be passed over without remark, though founded upon the strictest and justest (his own superlative) observation of nature. It was where Scudamour lies down to sleep in the cave of Care, and is constantly annoyed and roused by the graduated hammers of the old smith's men. He called for a copy of the F. Q., and, when it was brought, turned

---

[1] *notes of . . . to them*] Omitted by Raysor.

149

to the end of the Canto, where it is said that Scudamour at last, weary with his journey and his anxieties, fell asleep: Coleridge then read, with his peculiar intonation and swing of voice, the following stanza:—

> With that the wicked carle, the master Smith,
>   A paire of red-hot iron tongs did take
>   Out of the burning cinders, and therewith
>   Under his side him nipp'd; that, forc'd to wake,
>   He felt his hart for very paine to quake,
>   And started up avenged for to be
>   On him, the which his quiet slomber brake:
>   Yet looking round about him none could see;
> Yet did the smart remain, though he himself did flee.

'Having read this, Coleridge paused for a moment or two, and looked round with an inquiring eye, as much as to say, "Are you aware of what I refer to in this stanza?" Nobody saying a word, he went on: "I mean this—that at night, and in sleep, cares are not only doubly burdensome, but some matters, that then seem to us sources of great anxiety, are not so in fact; and when we are thoroughly awake, and in possession of all our faculties, they really seem nothing, and we wonder at the influence they have had over us. So Scudamour, while under the power and delusion of sleep, seemed absolutely nipped to the soul by the red-hot pincers of Care, but opening his eyes and rousing himself, he found that he could see nothing that had inflicted the grievous pain upon him: there was no adequate cause for the increased mental suffering Scudamour had undergone."

'The correctness of this piece of criticism was doubted, because in the last line it is said,

> Yet did the smart remain, though he himself did flee.

'Coleridge (who did not always answer objectors, but usually went forward with his own speculations) urged that although some smart might remain, it had not the same intensity:—that Scudamour had entered the cave in a state of mental suffering, and that what Spenser meant was, that sleep much enhanced and exaggerated that suffering; yet when Scudamour awoke, the cause of the increase was nowhere to be found. The original source of sorrow was not removed, but the red-hot pincers were removed, and there seemed no good reason for thinking worse of matters, than at the time the knight had fallen asleep. Coleridge enlarged for some time upon the reasons why distressing circumstances always seem doubly afflicting at night, when the body is in a horizontal position: he contended that the effect originated in the brain, to which the blood circulated with greater force and rapidity than when the body was perpendicular.

'The name of Samuel Rogers having been mentioned, a question arose how far he was entitled to the rank of a poet, and to what rank as a poet? My father produced a copy of "The Pleasures of Memory", which its author had given to him many years ago, before the termination of their intimacy . . .[1]

'Hazlitt contended that there was "a finical finish" (his own words) about the lines, which made them read like the composition of a mature period; and he added his conviction that they were produced with much labour and toil, and afterwards polished with painful industry. Such was indisputably the fact; and it was generally declared that no free and flowing poet could write so neat and formal a hand: it was fit for a banker's clerk, who was afterwards to become a banker. Coleridge dwelt upon the harmony and sweetness of many of the couplets, and was willing to put the versification about on a par with Goldsmith's "Traveller". Hazlitt, on the other hand, protested against Rogers being reckoned a poet at all: he was a banker; he had been born a banker, bred a banker, and a banker he must remain; if he were a poet, he was certainly a poet *sui generis*. "Aye, *sui generous* (stuttered Lamb, in his cheerful jocular way, looking at everything on the sunny and most agreeable side), Rogers is not like Catiline, *sui profusus*, any more than he is *alieni appetens*, but he is *sui generous*, and I believe that few deserving people make appeals to him in vain." This characteristic joke put everybody into good humour, and it was voted, almost *nem. con.*, that Rogers was a poet in spite of his purse;—"by virtue of it", added Hazlitt, and so the matter ended.'

There are[2] other particulars in my Diary, respecting Lord Byron (whose merits by the aid of the Edinburgh Review were then, I think, beginning to attract notice), Wordsworth, Crabbe, Southey, Moore, and others; but as it does not appear (and it would have appeared had such been the case) that Coleridge was present on any of these occasions, I refrain from giving them. The only exception I will make applies to indisputably the greatest name in the preceding enumeration—that of Wordsworth. The date under which I entered the following memorandum is 10th February, 1814, but it refers to an anterior period. It was

[1] *intimacy* . . .] The rest of this paragraph, on Rogers and Collier's father, is omitted (so Raysor).

[2] *There are* . . . *conversation*] Omitted by Raysor.

probably on one of those pleasant occasions, when my father received friends to tea and supper—the supper being served in at about eleven o'clock. I remember that not very unfrequently Coleridge, Wordsworth, Lamb and others, met together at these times, and that there was a great deal of lively literary and anecdotic conversation.[1] I wish I could recover some of the notes I made of what Coleridge told us, without any apparent reserve, of his early history; but I fear that they are irrecoverably lost.[2]

. . . to this day I have a grateful recollection of the patience, I may almost say indulgence, with which the great poet listened to me, then a young man, and, I must own, not by any means an unqualified admirer of of his poetry. Coleridge by his—(powers of conversation I cannot properly call them, but)—powers of speech, and a wonderfully attractive delivery,[3] had so taken possession of my mind, both as a poet and a critic, that Wordsworth had only a secondary place. I have since learned to estimate the last more justly. I then liked[4] him, not so much for what he

---

[1] *There are . . . conversation*] Omitted by Raysor.

[2] *lost*] I remember to this day that he told us the story of his short gown at college, which had been clipped and torn away, bit by bit, by his fellow-students. One day, meeting a proctor, that officer asked him, 'Mr. Coleridge, when do you mean to part with that gown?' Coleridge was a little proud of his ready reply— That it was an old friend; he was parting with it by degrees, and feared that, by the ill offices of others, the separation would soon be complete and final. He also gave us an account of what passed at Frend's trial, at Cambridge, when a one-armed man had suffered for clapping his hands, an offence which Coleridge had committed. According to my recollection, Coleridge was guilty of no duplicity, but the proctor of an unlucky blunder. He was not fond of alluding to his exploit of enlistment in the cavalry, under the name of Comberbach; but I heard him once mention it, with an allusion to the appropriateness of his pseudo-name, considering that he never could be taught to ride: as far as the horse was concerned, he was always a *cumberback*. On more than one occasion he adverted to the wild scheme of Southey, Lovel, and himself, with their three sister-wives, settling, I think, on the banks of the Chesapeake. To a late period of life, I believe, Coleridge maintained not only the feasibility, but the reasonableness of the plan in many respects (Collier's note). Collier goes on to report a conversation with Wordsworth, which Raysor prints, but which is omitted here as not relevant to Coleridge.

[3] *delivery*] I always thought his mouth beautiful: the lips were full, and a little drawn down at the corners, and when he was speaking the attention (at least my attention) was quite as much directed to his mouth as to his eyes, the expression of it was so eloquent. In the energy of talking, 'the rose-leaves' were at times 'a little bedewed', but his words seemed to flow the easier for the additional lubricity. I did not especially admire Coleridge's 'large grey eyes', for, now and then, they assumed a dead, dull look, almost as if he were not seeing out of them; and I doubt if external objects made much impression upon his sight, when he was animated in discourse (Collier's note).

[4] *I then liked . . . so still*] Omitted by Raysor.

had written, (the hyper-simplicity of which is even now not thoroughly relished by me) as for the admiration I had always heard Coleridge express of him. Long after the 'Lyrical Ballads' were published, I was much more in love with the two pieces by Coleridge, than with any other part of the production. I believe I am so still.[1]

I had not seen Wordsworth before Coleridge had delivered his Lectures of 1811–12; but afterwards I met him rather frequently, and I cannot say, as others have said in my company, that I was ever weary of listening to him, when (as he usually did) he talked about his own poetry. Whenever he was in town, I did what I could to get into his society, and by the date that Coleridge delivered his course of Lectures in 1818, I was upon pretty easy terms with him; but he was not a man with whom one could ever be as familiar and hilarious as with Charles Lamb.[2]

---

[1] *I then liked . . . so still*] Omitted by Raysor.

[2] *Lamb*] Raysor printed several further passages, relating to Coleridge in later years, but these are not relevant here.

Appendix B

Collier's manuscript diary and transcripts of the 1811-12 lectures

The manuscript, known as Folger MS. M.a. 219–28, consists of ten sewn gatherings or 'brochures' (as Collier called them in *Seven Lectures on Shakespeare and Milton*, xii). Eight are identical in size, the pages measuring seven-and-a-quarter inches by four inches, but the last two are slightly taller, measuring about seven-and-three-eighths inches by four inches. All have one gilt edge, as if they were designed to make a volume, or just possibly were broken up from a book, though there is no sign that they were ever bound. However, as Collier used them they were unbound, for Nos. 5, 7, 9 and 10 have to be reversed to put them in sequence so that the gilding appears on the top edge. The first four brochures are numbered 1 to 4 at the top left corner of the first page. The individual brochures are described below:

Brochure *1* (M.a. 219)

Thirty leaves. Pp. 1–2 are blank; pp. 3–4 contain a list of 'Contents'; pp. 5–58 (numbered 1–54) are filled with notes written in ink, headed 'Diary or Journal Thursday Oct 10th', and the year '1811' added in pencil; pp. 59–60 are blank. Several leaves are watermarked with the date 1811.

Brochure *2* (M.a. 220)

Twenty-six leaves. A copy of the printed prospectus of Coleridge's lectures of 1811–12 at the London Philosophical Society, commencing 18 November, is tipped in and attached to the first leaf; this is marked with the letter 'A' in the top left corner Pp. 1–2 list the 'Contents'; pp.

3–48 (numbered 55–102) continue the diary entries from Brochure 1. The last two pages are blank except for the word 'compares', which has been roughly deleted. There are no discernible watermarks, except in the printed prospectus, which is watermarked with the date 1811.

Brochure 3 (M.a. 221)

Twenty-eight leaves. The first page has the mark 'B', and the notation in ink by William Clark, Commissioner, that this is the diary 'referred to in the Affidavit of John Payne Collier sworn before me this eighth day of January 1856'. P. 2 is blank; p. 3 lists 'Contents'; pp. 4–6 are blank; pp. 7–54 (numbered 103–50) continue the entries from Brochure 2. Pp. 55–6 are blank, except for pencilled jottings in French on p. 56. There are no discernible watermarks. In the diary entry for Monday, 18th November, the day when Coleridge gave his first lecture of the series, Collier began to include 'the notes I took of the lecture' (pp. 143–50).

Brochure 4 (M.a. 222)

Twenty-eight leaves. P. 1 is headed 'Coleridge's First Lecture (conclusion) Second lecture (p. 157)'. P. 2 is blank; pp. 3–33 (numbered 151–77) continue the entries from Brochure 3. On p. 7 (157), within the entry for Thursday, 21st November, is the heading 'Second Lecture' The transcription of this lecture ends on p. 23 (173). On p. 26 (176), in the entry for Monday, 25th November, Collier noted that he heard Coleridge's third lecture, and transcribed his notes elsewhere. There are no discernible watermarks in this brochure. The diary entries come to an end in this brochure.

Brochure 5 (M.a. 223)

Twenty-four leaves. P. 1 is headed 'Coleridge's Sixth Lecture/Seventh D°'. P. 2 is blank; pp. 3–36 contain a transcript of Lecture 6; pages 37–46 contain the first part of Lecture 7. Pp. 47–8 are blank, except for the words 'of the' deleted. Several leaves are watermarked with the date 1807. The pages were not numbered by Collier.

Brochure 6 (M.a. 224)

Twenty-four leaves. Page 1 is headed 'End [Part] of Lect. 7/Beginning of Lect. 8'. P. 2 is blank; pp. 3–36 contain a transcript of Lecture 7, and pp. 37–46 contain the first part of Lecture 8. The last two pages are blank. Several leaves are watermarked with the date 1807. The pages were not numbered by Collier.

Brochure 7 (M.a. 225)

Twenty-four leaves. P. 1 is headed with a brief note in shorthand, and underneath is written 'End of Lecture 8 (not finished)'. The date '1772' has been pencilled in the top left corner. P. 2 is blank; pp. 3–24 contain the text of the lecture, and pp. 25–48 are blank. Many leaves are water-marked with the date 1807. The pages were not numbered by Collier.

Brochure 8 (M.a. 226)

Twenty-four leaves. P. 1 is headed '9th', and 'Coleridge's Ninth Lec-ture'. The date '1772' has been added in pencil. P. 2 is blank; pp. 3–46 contain the text of Lecture 9; pp. 47–8 are blank. One leaf is water-marked with the date 1807. The pages were not numbered by Collier.

Brochure 9 (M.a. 227)

Twenty-six leaves. P. 1 is headed '9th' and 'End of Lecture 9', and has the date '1772' pencilled in the top left corner. P. 2 is blank; pp. 3–11 contain the conclusion of Lecture 9; pp. 12–52 are blank. Several leaves are watermarked with the date 1806. The pages were not numbered by Collier.

Brochure 10 (M.a. 228)

Twenty-two leaves. P. 1 is headed 'Lecture 12', and has the date '1772' pencilled in the top left corner. P. 2 is blank; pp. 3–34 contain the text of the lecture. On p. 24 Collier turned the brochure sideways, and wrote from this point on across the length of the page; there is a change of ink, and the handwriting is more slanting and appears more rapid. Near the foot of p. 23 is a pencilled note, 'See Short-hand Note A', which refers to a corresponding mark in the surviving short-hand notes (see below, p. 159). Several leaves are watermarked with the date 1806. The pages were not numbered by Collier.

Collier's short-hand alphabet

The basic alphabet of Collier's short-hand is as follows:

b	`\`	n	`∪`	
c k q	`σ` or `ᴄ`	p	`⌐`	
d	`C`	r	`/`	
f	`ſ`	s z	`—`	
g	`℮` or `🔆`	t	`|`	
h	`9`	v	`P` or `ſ`	
j	`🔆`	w	`9` or `P`	
l	`6` or `9`	x	`6`	
m	`∩`	into	`d`	
~ion, ~ing	`—` or `…`	what	`Ɔ`	
with, that	`⌐` or `⌐`	which	`9`	
of the, to the	`…`	sh	`6`	
~ant, ent	`∪`	at	`1`	

Appendix C

Collier's short-hand notebooks

In the Affidavit of January 1856, printed in *Seven Lectures on Shake-speare and Milton*, Collier stated that after completing transcripts of them for his edition he destroyed the short-hand notes of his lectures, 'as being of no value, except the two now produced to me, and marked G and H, which are the original notes taken down by me, from the mouth of the said Samuel Taylor Coleridge, in the year 1811'.[1] So much is misreported or confused by Collier that it is rather surprising to find that this statement may be true. Two short-hand notebooks, containing the marks 'G' and 'H', and notes by William Clark certifying that they were produced to support Collier's affidavit, do apparently survive. I say apparently because I have not succeeded in locating the originals, which disappeared in the 1930s, when they were sold by an American scholar who then owned them.[2] However, in 1937 facsimiles were lodged in the Library of Congress and in the Folger Shakespeare Library in Washington, D.C. I have been able to use these, and, by courtesy of the Library of Congress, to reproduce two pages from them (see Plates 4 and 5).

Collier said in 1856 that he then transcribed parts of all the early lectures from his original short-hand notes, and claimed explicitly that two of the brochures of these notes, those of the ninth and twelfth lectures, had until then been 'completely untranscribed'.[3] This statement, I believe, is simply untrue. Lectures 9 and 12 are transcribed in the Folger manuscript, and the evidence indicates that these long-hand

---

[1] *Seven Lectures*, iv.

[2] They were owned by Professor Paul Kaufman of the University of Washington, Seattle, who no longer remembers who purchased them from him.

[3] *Seven Lectures*, iii, xii.

versions were written out soon after the lectures were delivered, in 1811 or 1812. There was, it seems, a break in the transcription of Lecture 12, where the pencilled comment, 'See Short-hand Note A' corresponds to a heavily marked and underlined 'A' in the short-hand notes in this lecture; but I think that only a short interval elapsed before Collier finished transcribing this lecture, for the rest of it is consonant in style with the first part, and the whole is consistently different from what he printed in 1856.[1] In fact, Collier did not in his *Seven Lectures* present a text of Lectures 9 and 12 transcribed from the short-hand notes; it is I think, possible to demonstrate this.

According to his own account,[2] Collier's father, who was a reporter, taught him short-hand 'at an early age'. This may help to account for a number of personal variants in his use of a system derived from John Byrom's *Universal English Short-hand* (1767), perhaps as popularized by T. Molineux in *An Introduction to Mr. Byrom's Universal English Short-Hand* (1804). Like many later systems of short-hand, this one is based on a representation of consonants by a variety of dashes and signs, with vowels registered intermittently, and indicated by dots. It has proved possible to work out the basic alphabet used by Collier, and to transcribe some of the notes.[3] To decipher them is a very difficult task, except where they agree pretty well with Collier's own long-hand transcription, which helps to clarify obscurities and ambiguities. For a group of consonants may indicate a variety of words, as, for example, 'mns' may represent 'immense', 'means', 'mines', 'moans', 'mince', 'manse', and no doubt other words too. A series of such ambiguities in a passage can render it impenetrable, and I have not yet succeeded in deciphering all of the notes. Fortunately, they correspond for the most part fairly closely to the text of the long-hand transcripts.

The notes I have deciphered sufficiently establish that the long-hand transcriptions made soon after the lectures were given, and printed for the first time in this volume, are based on the short-hand notes, and represent a polished version of them. Collier seems to have amplified and corrected from memory what he set down in the course of the lecture, and since he did this soon after the lectures were delivered, the text of his early transcriptions may be presumed to be close, usually very close, to what Coleridge actually said. However, he occasionally omitted a

---

[1] See above, p. 123 and n.

[2] *Seven Lectures*, v.

[3] I am greatly indebted in this to Mr F. Higenbotham, the City Librarian of Canterbury, who deciphered most of the characters for me, and who has generously helped me out of his expert knowledge of antiquarian short-hand.

phrase or sentence which makes no sense, or altered a rather incomprehensible note to make sense of it. His short-hand does not appear to have been expert enough to enable him to take down everything Coleridge said, but clearly he did take down some passages verbatim. I would guess that he was also forced to skip whole sentences at times, or take them down in such a garbled form that he could not afterwards reconstruct them; indeed, he said:

> I did not knowingly register a sentence, that did not come from Coleridge's lips, although doubtless I missed, omitted, and mistook points and passages, which now I should have been most rejoiced to have preserved. In completing my transcripts, however, I have added no word or syllable of my own.[1]

The first part of this statement is almost certainly true. The last sentence is quite certainly untrue. For even if Collier added no words of his own in his early transcriptions of the short-hand notes, he clearly did so in the text he published in 1856. This text is based on the long-hand transcriptions, not the short-hand notes, and in it Collier expanded freely, altered references and quotations, and rewrote many sentences. So in the passage cited below from Lecture 9, Collier added in 1856 the name 'Lopez de Vega', which is not in the short-hand notes, or in the early transcription, or for that matter in the part of Schlegel's Lecture XII to which Coleridge was alluding here. Schlegel did elsewhere in his lectures comment at length on Lope de Vega, and Collier may have added the reference for this reason. The reader who cares to compare the texts as set out below will find other examples which show that in 1856 Collier followed, but altered and adapted at will, the early long-hand transcript of Lecture 9. These two texts tend to agree at points where both differ from the short-hand notes. The example printed here of what can be recovered, with great labour and some uncertainty, from two of the clearer pages of the short-hand notes, also serves to show, in my opinion, that the best text we have of these lectures is that of the early transcript in the Folger manuscript. It is true that this omits some phrases and sentences of the short-hand notes, probably because Collier himself could not make sense at these points, and there is little reason to suppose that we can now adequately reconstruct what Coleridge was saying. At the same time, the early transcripts, made, if I am right, when the lectures were fresh in Collier's mind, fill out the short-hand notes with what he recollected, and provide us with the best text avail-

---

[1] *Seven Lectures*, vi–vii.

able, even if it does not at all points offer the very words Coleridge spoke. It is impossible to know what Collier thought he was doing when he published *Seven Lectures* in 1856, but he may have felt that he ought to present Coleridge suitably arranged for Victorian readers, and saw no reason why he should not rewrite the records he had himself made more than forty years earlier. I do not understand why he claimed to be transcribing his short-hand notes for the first time, for by the 1850s these must have been almost as hard to recover as they are now. At best they provide a rough outline, and for this to be filled out the power of recall available to the transcriber only within a short period of hearing the speaker was clearly necessary. The Folger manuscript provides just such a filling-out of the short-hand notes, and it was from this transcript that Collier elaborated his text in 1856.

Three versions of part of the text of Lecture 9 are presented here, so that a ready comparison can be made between them. The first is a transcription, as accurate as I can make it, of pp. 2 and 3 of the short-hand notes of this lecture. No doubt I have made mistakes in decipher-ing this, but the pages are interesting as containing one or two sentences Collier evidently took down in an abbreviated or garbled form. I have kept the paragraphing of the notes; these have no punctuation, and I have added only full-stops and capitals to mark what seem to be sen-tences. The second reprints the text from the long-hand transcripts, as given above on pp. 99–101. It will be noticed that some phrases appear in this for which there is no hint in the short-hand notes, and that some sentences are rearranged or expanded. Here I believe Collier was adding and altering from his recollections of what Coleridge said, so that the additions can be accepted as authentic, or at least as recording the sense of Coleridge's words. He also omitted entirely from the transcript one incomprehensible sentence, which perhaps puzzled him to such a degree that he could not recall what Coleridge meant; it is also possible that Coleridge was incomprehensible at this point. The third version is the text as printed by Collier in 1856. This contains numerous expansions of and additions to the text of the early transcript, but is clearly based on this. It also omits some phrases or sentences that appear in the transcript, and one phrase ('with what, out of his mixed nature, he cannot produce') which appears only in the early transcript. This is the only point at which the 1856 text and the short-hand notes coincide against the long-hand transcript, and it is in the case of a phrase that fails to appear in either. Since Collier omitted other phrases in 1856, and since everywhere else the 1856 text is developed from the long-hand transcript, it seems to me unlikely that Collier troubled himself much, if at all, about the short-hand notes in preparing the text for *Seven Lectures*.

1 *The text in the short-hand notebooks, Lecture 9, pp. 2 and 3*
mentioned as dramatic poems consider that the ancient drama might be contrasted with the Shakespearian call that Shakespearian because knew no other author who so realized the same idea though told Calderon has done that.

They might be compared to the others and in the same manner as painting to statuary. The figures must be few because the very essence of statuary is great abstraction and prevent great many being being [sic] combined into one effect. Consider a grand group of Niobe or an old heroic subject. Suppose the old Nurse were introduced that would be disgusting. The numbers must circumscribed and nothing undignified must be brought into company with what is dignified and no one of the group can be known but what is abstraction and nothing by the eye and figure which gives the effect of multitude without introducing anything discordant. This compare the picture of Raphael or Titian where immense number of figures may be introduced the dog cat and beggar and by the very circumstance less degree of labour and by less degree of abstraction effect is produced equally harmonious to the mind more true to nature and in all but one respect superior to statuary. A man to effect the perfect of satisfaction in a thing as a work of art.

He wholly felt it that exquisite feeling in imperfect being mighty preface of his future existence being holy is often that object presented to him.

What the reason conceives possible gives momentary reality to it.

Stated before the circumstances which permitted Shakespeare to make an alteration so suitable to his age and so necessitated by the circumstances of the age. In the ancient theatres the plays were composed for the whole stage the voice distorted by it.

The distinction between imitation and likeness is the mixture of a greater number of dissimilarities with the similarities.

p. 3
An imitation differs from a copy precisely as sameness differs from likeness in that sense of the word in which we imply a difference conjoined with that sameness.

Shakespeare had many advantages. The great then instead of throwing the chevaux de frise round them of mere manners endeavoured to distinguish themselves by attainments and powers of mind.

The poet was obliged to appeal to the imagination and not to the senses and that gave him a power over space and time which in the ancient theatre would have been absurd simply because it was contradictory.

The advantage is vast indeed on the side of the modern. He appeals to the imagination to the reason and to the noblest powers of the human heart above the iron compulsion of space and time. He appeals to that which we most want to be when we are most worthy of being while the other binds us often to the meanest part of our nature and its chief compensation is a simple cold acquiescence of the mind that what the poet has represented might possibly have taken place. A poor compliment to the poet who is to be a creator to tell him he has all the excellences of a historian. But in dramatic that so narrows the space of action so impoverishes the state of art that of all the Athenian dramas scarcely no one which has not fallen into absurdity by aiming at the thing and failing or incurred greater absurdity by bringing things into the same space of time that could not have occurred. Not to mention that the grandest effect of the dramatic poet to be the mirror of life is completely lost. The passing in 6 or 12 hours though this depicted 24 hours though in fact we might have supposed that as easily 20 months as 20 hours because it has become an object of imagination and when

p. 4
once the bound is passed there is no limit which can be appointed it.

2 *The text in the early long-hand transcript*
mentioned as dramatic poems) might be contrasted with the Shakespearian Drama: he had called it Shakespearian, because he knew no other writer who had realized the same idea, although he had been told that the Spanish Poet Calderon had been as successful. The Shakespearian drama and the Greek drama might be compared to painting and statuary. In the latter, as in the Greek drama, the characters must be few, because the very essence of statuary was a high degree of abstraction, which would prevent a great many figures from being combined into the same effects. In a grand group of Niobe, or any other ancient heroic subject, how disgusting it would appear were an old nurse introduced. The numbers must be circumscribed, and nothing undignified must be brought into company with what is dignified; no one personage must be brought in but what is abstraction: all must not be presented to the eye, but the effect of multitude must be produced without the introduction of anything discordant.

Compare this group with a picture by Raphael or Titian—where an immense number of figures might be introduced, even a dog, a cat, or a beggar, and from the very circumstance of a less degree of labour and a less degree of abstraction, an effect is produced equally harmonious to the mind, more true to nature, and in all respects but one superior to Statuary; the perfect satisfaction in a thing as a work of art. The man of taste feels satisfied with what, out of his mixed nature, he cannot produce, and to that which the reason conceives possible a momentary reality was given, by the aid of the imagination.

He had before stated the circumstances which permitted Shakespeare to make an alteration so suitable to his age, and so necessitated by the circumstances of the age. Coleridge here repeated what he had before said regarding the distortion of the human voice by the size of the ancient theatres, and the attempt introduced of making everything on the stage appear reality. The difference between an imitation and a likeness is the mixture of a greater number of circumstances of dissimilarity with those of similarity: an imitation differs from a copy precisely as sameness differs from likeness in that sense of the word in which we imply a difference conjoined with that sameness.

Shakespeare had likewise many advantages: the great at that time, instead of throwing round them the Chevaux de frise of mere manners, endeavoured to distinguish themselves by attainments, by energy of thought, and consequent powers of mind. The stage had nothing but curtains for its scenes, and the Actor as well as the author were obliged to appeal to the imagination, and not to the senses, which gave the latter a power over space and time which in the ancient theatre would have been absurd simply because it was contradictory. The advantage is indeed vastly on the side of the modern: he appeals to the imagination, to the reason, and to the noblest powers of the human heart: he is above the iron compulsion of space and time. He appeals to that which we most wish to be when we are most worthy of being, while the ancient dramas bind us down to the meanest part of our nature, and its chief compensation is a simple acquiescence of the mind that what the Poet has represented might possibly have taken place—a poor compliment to a Poet who is to be a creator, to tell him that he has all the excellences of a historian! In dramatic composition, the Unities of Time and Place so narrowed the space of action, and so impoverished the sources of pleasure, that of all the Athenian dramas there is scarcely one which has not fallen into absurdity by aiming at an object and failing, or which has not incurred greater absurdity by bringing events into a space of time in which it is impossible for them to have happened; not to mention that the grandest effort of the Dramatist to be the mirror of life is completely lost.

The limit allowed by the Greeks was 24 hours, but we might as well take 24 months, because it has already become an object of imagination. The mind is then acted upon by such strong stimulants that the one and the other are indifferent; when once the limit of possibility is passed there are no bounds which can be assigned to imagination.

3 *The text as printed in* Seven Lectures on Shakespeare and Milton *(1856), pp. 95–9 (Raysor, II, 159–61 (122–4))*
treated as original theatrical poems) might be contrasted with the Shakespearian drama.—I call it the Shakespearean drama to distinguish it, because I know of no other writer who had realised the same idea, although I am told by some, that the Spanish poets, Lopez de Vega and Calderon, have been equally successful. The Shakespearean drama and the Greek drama may be compared to statuary and painting. In statuary, as in the Greek drama, the characters must be few, because the very essence of statuary is a high degree of abstraction, which prevents a great many figures being combined in the same effect. In a grand group of Niobe, or in any other ancient heroic subject, how disgusting even it would appear, if an old nurse were introduced. Not only the number of figures must be circumscribed, but nothing undignified must be placed in company with what is dignified: no one personage must be brought in that is not an abstraction: all the actors in the scene must not be presented at once to the eye; and the effect of multitude, if required, must be produced without the intermingling of anything discordant.

Compare this small group with a picture by Raphael or Titian, in which an immense number of figures may be introduced, a beggar, a cripple, a dog, or a cat; and by a less degree of labour, and a less degree of abstraction, an effect is produced equally harmonious to the mind, more true to nature with its varied colours, and, in all respects but one, superior to statuary. The man of taste feels satisfied, and to that which the reason conceives possible, a momentary reality is given by the aid of imagination.

I need not here repeat what I have said before, regarding the circumstances which permitted Shakespeare to make an alteration, not merely so suitable to the age in which he lived, but, in fact, so necessitated by the condition of that age. I need not again remind you of the difference I pointed out between imitation and likeness, in reference to the attempt to give reality to representations on the stage. The distinction between imitation and likeness depends upon the admixture of circumstances of dissimilarity; an imitation is not a copy, precisely as likeness is not sameness, in that sense of the word 'likeness' which implies difference conjoined with sameness. Shakespeare reflected manners in his plays, not by a cold formal copy, but by an imitation: that is to say, by an admixture of circumstances, not absolutely true in themselves, but true to the character and to the time represented.

It is fair to own that he had many advantages. The great of that day, instead of surrounding themselves by the *chevaux de frise* of what is now called high breeding, endeavoured to distinguish themselves by attainments, by energy of thought, and consequent powers of mind. The stage, indeed, had nothing but curtains for its scenes, but this fact compelled the actor, as well as the author, to appeal to the imaginations, and not to the senses of the audience: thus was obtained a power over space and time, which in an ancient theatre would have been absurd, because it would have been contradictory. The advantage is vastly in favour of our own early stage: the dramatic poet there relies upon the imagination, upon the reason, and upon the noblest powers of the human heart; he shakes off the iron bondage of space and time; he appeals to that which we most wish to be, when we are most worthy of being, while the ancient dramatist binds us down to the meanest part of our nature, and the chief compensation is a simple acquiescence of the mind in the position, that what is represented might possibly have occurred in the time and place required by the unities. It is a poor compliment to a poet to tell him, that he has only the qualifications of a historian.

In dramatic composition the observation of the unities of time and place so narrows the period of action, so impoverishes the sources of pleasure, that of all the Athenian dramas there is scarcely one in which the absurdity is not glaring, of aiming at an object, and utterly failing in the attainment of it: events are sometimes brought into a space in which it is impossible for them to have occurred, and in this way the grandest effort of the dramatist, that of making his play the mirror of life, is entirely defeated.

The limit allowed by the rules of the Greek stages was twenty-four hours: but, inasmuch as, even in this case, time must have become a subject of imagination, it was just as reasonable to allow twenty-four months, or even years. The mind is acted upon by such strong stimulants, that the period is indifferent; and when once the boundary of possibility is passed, no restriction can be assigned.

Index

Index

Dixon, W. H., 7
Dow, Gerard, 79
Drummond, William, 25, 68
Dryden, John, 70, 74, 78–9, 126,
  135, 139
Dyce, Alexander, 8
Dyer, George, 60, 134
  conversation reported, 61–2

Edinburgh Review, 151
Elegant Extracts, 61
Elwes, John, 87
Emlyn, Sollom, 40
Euclid, 56
Euripides, 22–3, 99, 139

Fairfax, Edward, 141, 142
Falstaff, 30–1, 72, 116, 130
Fata Morgana, 21, 102
Field, Nathaniel, 131
Fielding, Henry, *Tom Jones*, 80
Fletcher, John, *see also* Beaumont,
  Francis, 74, 84, 133
Frend, William, 152
Friedman, Arthur, 51n.

Galileo, 139
Garrick, David, 135
Gibbon, Edward, 3
Gifford, William, 71n.
Gillman, James, 8
Godwin, William, 2, 30, 130
Goethe, J. W. von, 139
Goldsmith, Oliver, 51, 58, 151
Gray, Thomas, 69
Gresset, Jean Baptiste Louis, 140
Gulliver's Travels, 53

Halliday, —, 63
Halliwell, J. O., 8
Harington, Sir John, 141
Hartley, David, 139
Hatton, Christopher, Viscount, 46
Haydn, Joseph, 56n.
Hazlitt, William, 2, 60, 134, 140,
  141, 142, 151
  comments on Coleridge, 61–3
Herculaneum, excavations, 98

Herodotus, 139
Herschel, Sir William, 34, 55n.,
  137
Higenbotham, F., ix, 159n.
Hobbes, Thomas, 139
Homer, 65–6, 139, 140
Hooker, Richard, 26, 90–1, 139
Husson, Henri-Marie, 37

Ingleby, C. M., 8–9, 10n., 12

Jeffrey, Richard, 42n.
Johnson, Dr. Samuel, 4, 38, 44, 59,
  61, 62–3, 78–9, 102, 119, 121n.,
  127–8
  Vanity of Human Wishes, 62,
  70
Jonson, Ben, 56n., 134
Juvenal, 63, 70

Kant, Immanuel, 36, 139
Kaufman, Paul, 19n., 158n.
Ker, W. P., 74n., 78n.
Kotzebue, August von, 32, 135
Krusve, Bernard, 103

Lamb, Charles, 2, 5, 6, 31, 37, 51,
  60, 103n., 134, 140, 141, 142,
  145, 149, 151, 152, 153
  comments on Coleridge, 61–3
Lamb, Mary, 60, 134, 141
Lancaster, Joseph, 64n.
Lewis, M. G. 'Monk', 25, 73
Livy, 139
Lloyd, Charles, 134
Locke, John, 36, 38–9, 138
London Philosophical Society,
  154
Lonsdale, Earl of, 36–7
Lovell, Robert, 152n.
Lowther, Sir James, *see* Lonsdale,
  Earl of
Lucas, E. V., 103n.
Lytton, Bulwer, 145

Malone, Edmund, 131
  1821 edition of Shakespeare,
  18–19, 121n., 123n., 127
Massinger, Philip, 71, 72